Home Front

A Memoir from WW II

C. D. Peterson

eISBN: 9781940773421
Print ISBN: 9781940773438

For all those who experienced life on the home front
So some can remember, more will learn, and none may forget

ACKNOWLEDGEMENTS

My sincere thanks to all those "last ones" who contributed their experiences on the war time home front to my website. Their encouragement and enthusiasm kept me going. A special nod to members of my Naval Aviation Cadet Class 44-1956 who were among the first to step up.

Donaugh Bracken, my publisher at History Publishing, exhibited great patience with my need to protect my story.

I am indebted to my family and friends for their support and understanding of my unconventional, and often annoying, writing habits.

And as always, to Odessa, Wendy, Stephanie, and Chris.

Cover design:
Stephen Roth, Roth Graphics

Cover art:
Shelley Lowell

Interior sketches:
Betty Ann Medeiros

PREFACE

People write memoirs out of need—perhaps out of a need for therapy, to quench a vanity, or to satisfy an adoring public. My need is to create a legacy, not a personal legacy for my descendants, but a legacy for a small cohort of a special generation. Any urgency detected in my writing is driven by my awareness that I am among "the last ones."

Born in the 1930s, we are the last ones who personally experienced the scarcity of the Depression, the fear and patriotism during World War II, and the exuberance in that brief, pretelevision, postwar period when we felt safe and when the middle class was born.

After the war, with the GI Bill, VA loans, and fully stocked store shelves, the country was all about getting back to normal. But for some, normal was gone.

This memoir is about my New England farm family and about how normal evaded our reach.

. . . .

Critics propound incompatible rules about memoirs: you can exaggerate, you can conflate, you can transpose, you can change names and places, you can omit, you can time jump, you can forget, you can even imagine and suppose conversations, but you can't lie, except for narrative purposes.

Though many of these events are more than seventy years gone, I have followed those rules.

C. D. Peterson
November 2017

. . . .

Special Notes

"In 1926 the state flooded Prescott Valley under water to develop the big Quabbin reservoir so they could bring water to people in Boston. They took our farm. Your grandmother, your father, and I—your uncle Carl was just a *liten pojke*—drove our cows down the car roads here to Framingham to make Hillcrest Farm. The newspapers took pictures. They called it a cattle drive."

Grandfather Enoch Peterson
Said to me when I was a boy

"Developers have obtained the 150 acre Hillcrest Farm in Framingham. The farm lies along the Massachusetts Turnpike Authority's developing westward route. In addition to a major highway interchange, plans for the property include an industrial center and a critical bridge over the reservoir system that supplies water to Boston. Hillcrest Farm had been owned and operated as a dairy farm since 1926 by Enoch and Myrtle Peterson and their family."

Framingham News, June 1955

PART ONE

LIFE DURING THE WAR

INTRODUCTION

December 7th, 1941, is the earliest memory I can swear to. To me, it seemed as though a second world had been layered on us. Everything we did now had an added meaning; we didn't just farm, we farmed for the war effort. We sang extra songs in school for our boys overseas. "Make do!" was the slogan, and rationing was the reality. Save tin. Save fat. Save paper. A long feared storm had arrived.

Separation and longing swelled into the center of our lives. In movies and magazines, I saw visions of the war. I learned the names Roosevelt and Hitler and places like Iwo Jima and Monte Casino.

I felt, as we all did, the bonding and camaraderie of the shared threat with my schoolmates, neighbor farmers, and even strangers brushing by on the street. Patriotism, and its inverse otherness of our enemies, showed itself in signs and slogans.

Children fared variously, with some sending fathers into the war and some also sending mothers into factories. Some had great fear, feeling we would always be at war. We had no agency. We watched; dependent, impotent, and obliged to be silent. We started growing our lives and waited for things to get better.

I fared well and felt I did my part.

. . . .

I heard the car brake hard out on the state highway and then turn in right behind us on the river road. Scratch and I hadn't walked a minute down the dirt road—really a tractor path of dirt strips with grass in the middle. The dark-green car slowed in the ruts and stopped short of us. The car engine went quiet. A tall man wearing a white shirt swung out and stood to look at me, like he was thinking about what to do next. Then he walked toward me smiling, slow steps, head to one side, like you come up to a shy calf.

He stopped a few paces away, pulled out a floppy handkerchief, and wiped his glasses. "Going fishing?" he asked as he resettled his glasses on his nose.

Scratch went and sniffed the man's cuff and came back to stand by me. "Yes," I said, thinking it pretty obvious, seeing as how I was walking the dirt road toward the water and carrying a pole, but I knew adults asked kids obvious questions to get them talking.

He took another slow step into my shade under the tunnel of butternut trees. His shirt was damp. He folded his hands in front of his waist and said, "My name is Gordon Emory. May I talk to you for a few minutes?" I told him yes, and he peppered me all about what I did: What's my name, how old am I, where do I fish, what do I catch, what's my dog's name, is that my dairy farm up there, and other things like that. He kept smiling and looking over his shoulder at a blonde woman sitting in his big car. She had her window down and was smiling, too.

When he seemed to run out of questions, he said, "Thank you, Douglas. It's been nice to meet you." He said he thought to go up and talk with my folks for a while. He backed a few steps, turned, and walked to his car, saying something to the woman that made her laugh, but I couldn't hear what he said. The car tires threw up grass and dust as he crunched a turn and drove out to the four-lane state road and off toward the farm. I saw the blonde woman looking back at me and smiling the whole time. I wondered what I had done to make them happy like that.

Scratch and I watched them drive out of sight and then set back walking down Brewer Road. The road didn't really have a name, but it led over to Brewer's farm, and so it got called that. It also led out to a good spot to fish—a small cove full of lily pads. I spent my afternoon fishing and wondering about the man and the blonde woman. After I finished fishing, Scratch and I walked home by the back way, over our big hill, and when I topped out, I could see down the far away stocky figure of my grandmother stationed in the farmyard. The only reason she would stand out there was to watch for me.

When I reached the yard, she came near to collect my fish. "You had a talk with some strangers," she said. I nodded yes. "They were from the Ford Motor Company," she announced. "They came up here and wanted to know all about you and the farm. It seems Ford puts out a magazine that tells about things from all over the country, and you are going to be in it. They saw you and Scratch walking the dirt road and wanted to tell about a boy on a New England farm."

I didn't see much reason to do that, but she said we couldn't pretend to know why people do what they do.

In September our RFD lady, Janice, a hulk of a woman, dropped off a cardboard carton of *Ford Times* magazines. The story about me was called, "Meet Tom Sawyer." It told all about me on our farm and how I hung out at the river with a stick fishing pole and didn't wear shoes and had a spotted pointer named Scratch. It even told how my grandmother made me wear a whistle around my neck so when she rang the barn bell and I whistled back she would know I was OK. Everyone around agreed it was a good story even though they left out the part that I was a daydreamer and always late coming up for chores.

The story also told how the farm got started. It said that my grandfather came from Sweden with his two sisters and four brothers and went to work at the Waltham Watch Company. My grandmother grew up in Maine and got sent to Boston to become a nurse. The story told how he didn't like being a watchmaker and she didn't like being a nurse so, in 1915, they set out for the Berkshires in Western Massachusetts where they bought a small farm. My father and my Uncle Carl were born in Prescott. It told how they farmed there for twelve years until the state flooded the valley and took the farm, making the Quabbin Reservoir to send water to the people in Boston. In 1926, the four of them drove their two dozen Guernsey dairy cows, cattle drive-style, twenty-five miles to Framingham, where they found this farm that had a big birch hill on it, next to the river. They put up a white sign with black letters: "Hillcrest Farm."

My grandmother mailed a copy of the *Ford Times* to her mother down East.

. . . .

I knew the water that went around our farm wasn't really a river like they said in the *Ford Times*. It made up part of the connection of reservoirs that flowed from the big Quabbin reservoir to the people in Boston. It did have a distinct—but slow—flow, and after the story called me Tom Sawyer, I always thought of that water as my Mississippi River. The same summer as the Ford people came by, I tried to leap like Superman from the hayloft into a stack of loose hay. I sprained my wrist and needed a cast for two weeks. My grandmother said how I wasn't tethered to the world quite tight and that it seemed any stray wisp of fantasy could carry me off.

. . . .

Once, when I was little, we got slammed with a wild thunderstorm raging with lightning flashes. We stood, sheltered, behind a curtain of rain in the barn doorway—my father, my grandfather, and I—talking about all the lightning and about the safest place to be during a lightning storm. "I bet the safest place is in the stone basement in the house," I guessed. "No," my father said, "it's in a car." My grandfather nodded strong assent. "The rubber tires are insulation, and lightning can't pass through the rubber." I didn't completely grasp the science of it, but it sounded to me like rubber could protect me from lightning. The next time a storm hit, I looked for some rubber to protect me and chose the rubber eraser tips on the pencils at my grandmother's desk. I figured how if I ate the rubber erasers, I would be protected. It took no time for my grandmother to call me in about the chewed-off tips. When I explained my reason, she told me how we were extra safe because her father had come from down Maine a long time ago to put up the best lightning rods he could build on all our buildings, even the silo.

She said if I ever felt afraid of things, I should come to her.

. . . .

"If the Japanese win any more battles, they could win all the way to California," I heard my grandmother say. She sat at the scarred oak desk that served as the hub of our farm and to which everything else seemed to be attached, scowling past our only telephone. I was getting some rye hard tack from the cold pantry, and I felt sure I shouldn't be listening, so I slipped out to be with our men in the dairy.

A few days before, I had overheard the men talking about how all the Japanese out West were being rounded up and sent out to the desert. This day, slapping their boots around the wet cement floor and rinsing everything down with chlorine water, Bob and Dick were talking about when they planned to go in. They decided to enlist rather than wait for the draft and guessed that they could be on their way pretty soon. My father and two uncles were already off in the Navy. With Bob and Dick heading off, that left just my grandparents, my mother, Uncle Carl, and me to handle the farm, and my mother wasn't a real farmer though she worked hard.

The newspapers had predicted that with the shortages, and how fast prices were going up, we would soon be rationed. Rationing began in January 1942—first with tires, then cars, then gasoline. We had ration stickers for gasoline and owned a yellow Minneapolis Moline tricycle front tractor with good rubber tires, but my grandfather figured we had better see if Tom and Jerry could still take to harness. He always talked about getting rid of the old Belgian buckskin team but never got around to it.

They turned out to be still workable for haying, if you rested them now and then. "Sure is quiet without that tractor roar," my grandfather said the first time we took them back out.

Gypsy, our riding horse, stood big enough to pull a wagon. Uncle Carl could build anything, and when the war started, he took an old cart bed and built it into a pretty good milk wagon. He painted it shiny red, white, and blue. We didn't use it a lot, but my mother did deliver milk with it, and the newspaper took her picture. "Well, look at you in the newspaper," my grandmother said.

"You're famous," my grandfather teased.

My mother was very young and looked it. One day, she came to take me out of school, and the teacher wouldn't hand me over until I peeped through the window in the door and said as how she was my mother.

Her name was Aida and people called her Edie. She had pretty, dark-brown hair and liked being tall.

Her two brothers enlisted in the navy right after Pearl Harbor. She had two sisters, Esther and Theresa, both with lots of kids, who lived in town. She went to see them every few days, and there was always something going on. Sometimes someone fell sick; sometimes a sister needed a ride; and now, with the war, she had to help out even more. Esther went to work at the rubber factory. My mother sometimes stayed for a couple of days.

· · · · · · · · · · · · · · · · ·

Every farm out by us sent men to the war and had run up against shortages of all kinds, and so old Mr. Brewer got all the farmers together to work out a plan. We met inside his big, green farm stand; it smelled of sour cider. It was the first time I ever sat in a grown-up meeting, and I felt nervous. Everyone was standing around the sorting table under hanging naked light bulbs. I drank coffee with lots of milk and sugar, and I heard people call my grandmother "Boss" and my grandfather "Pop." We had the newest dairy and ran it only half a day, so we agreed to take on pasteurizing milk from some of the smaller farms and putting it up in their bottles. In low voices, the farmers parceled out all the milk trucks, delivery men, tractors, and gasoline to make the most of them and agreed to help each other out with chores. Haying was tough because everybody needed to do it at the same time.

Walter Brewer, the oldest one there, said to Pop, "Good thing you didn't send your two Belgian pets to the glue factory." I saw smiles but heard no laughing.

Outside after the meeting, another farmer, Mr. Rawlings, asked me how old was I now, and I told him eight going on nine. Then he said, "With this war going on, you'll be a man before your mother." I felt good. Some of our men used that same joke on me when I did some big job, so I knew it meant that I was growing up.

In the meeting, some farmers had asked Pop if I could help on their milk routes. It wasn't like a regular job every day, only when I could, to help make the routes go faster now that they were all combined so big. My father used to be in charge of all our milk routes, so I knew how to help. They called a boy who did that a "striker."

Drivers always teased their strikers. When the drivers were putting on their uniforms and loading up out on the cement dock behind the cooler, one would call out, "Who's your striker today?"

Another would answer back, "I got Douglas so we'll be late. All the old women come out and give him cookies."

I needed to be a better striker than anyone, so I ran fast up to the house doors and leaped back on the truck before I even reached it. I had big hands and could carry six glass bottles at a time, but some boys were strong and could carry a whole case. The drivers had fun making us show who was best.

Striking on the milk routes meant more work on top of the extra farm work Pop and I had to do. Besides needing to relearn how to use horses, we had to learn how to save grease in cans, how to peel tinfoil, save metal parts, and wrap stacks of paper and cardboard to put out for collection on the state road. A white-painted table in the kitchen got given over as a station to manage our ration books, different-colored stamps, and the alphabet stickers we needed to buy gas and other things. Once every two weeks, my mother got dressed up and went into town to the gray War Memorial Building to sit on the ration board. When she came home, she told us about how some people tried to cheat, and some were hoarding. Our draft board kept its office in the same office building, and so sometimes when she came home she told us about men called "draft dodgers" who pretended to be sick to get out of serving in the war.

"Tom Barron is no more 4F than the man in the moon. Flat feet, he says." It surprised me that people were doing bad things during a war.

It was no surprise to anyone that I won the Victory Garden contests. The Boss had overseen me and our big vegetable garden ever since I could work a toy shovel and hoe. She liked to take pictures of me and my garden with her box camera. With mostly just me and Pop to do the farming work, I found I could handle Tom and Jerry pulling a white-birch brush harrow and I learned some plowing. I knew from the beginning that I did real work. I always believed what we did, farming, sat at the center of life. People had farmed forever - planting seeds, growing crops, raising cattle—and I felt I was a real part of it. I owned an important place in the world, especially now.

. . . .

Early mornings had me up and right out to the barn with Pop. The barn stood like an island of warm light in the dark yard, especially in winter when the stars were icy, and I crunched on the snow from one warm place to another. I loved the smells and sounds of the cows all rattling and shuffling around trying to look at us. If it had been very cold overnight, I would break the thin ice on each cow's water bowl, though most of the time they were strong enough to push down on the metal nose floats to get the water flowing. My first morning job was to bust open some bales of hay and lay a few sections in front of each cow. Next, I would clatter the wooden-wheeled grain cart down the aisle between the two stanchion rows of cows and dump a hand scoop of grain on the hay in front of each one. Pop pointed out any of the cows that needed some extra. Sometimes a cow nudged my hand, and I'd toss a little extra on my own.

We fed our cows different feed depending on the season and on what we had. Feeding the cows made up one of my main jobs. The cows did pasture graze, and we farmed our own hay, too. We also fed silage made from corn we grew, chopped, and blew into our silo. I liked feeding the cows their grain and their molasses that we kept in a sticky sweet, brown barrel on its side in the grain room. Feeding them molasses was easy; I just dipped a stick in the molasses bucket I carried and dribbled it on the feed in front of each cow. Silage took the most work. During the summer when we hooked up the small Minneapolis Moline to cut and blow the corn up into the silo, I owned the nasty job of working inside the stifling silo chamber under the dense-falling silage. I had to rake it around evenly and tromp on the wet mess to pack it down. As summer went on, the early, deep silage started to ferment, and the inside of the silo smelled like bad

8

whiskey. The men teased me about getting drunk in there, and Pop always made me climb down between loads.

To feed the silage, I had to climb up the ladder on the outside of the silo. The ladder—actually a set of removable blocks with a rung on each one—ran up the outside of the silo and was covered over by a metal chute. I shoveled the silage down the chute into a big, wheeled cart. Every week or so, as the level of the silage went down, I removed a block with its rung and placed it in an empty slot above me. My boots were always wet from the silage, and that made them slippery on the metal ladder rungs. I learned to lean back into the chute to brace myself as I climbed down, and I figured always to keep one hand on a rung.

My grandfather stood six feet tall. Slender and not a tough-looking man, he was very fit and extraordinarily strong.

Our bull owned a sour disposition and weighed close to a ton. Pop handled the animal in the bull pen's close quarters with ease, tugging at the ring in the bull's nose with a short, hooked rod. I feared for him, but he never showed concern. He worked the grueling farm hours and days with no hint of fatigue. He showed a certain joy swinging the two-handed scythe in his slow, arcing rhythm. Pop's motions were well oiled and seemed timeless, like he had made them forever

He started his morning work by wiping down the cows' udders with a burlap bag. At a steady pace, he shifted three milking machines down the row of cows. First he tossed a wide strap over the cow, reached underneath to hook it together loosely, and then hung the milking machine on the strap. After connecting a small hose to the vacuum line overhead, he pushed the cow's teats into the rubber-lined suction tubes. When he finished machine-milking a cow, he pulled up his three-legged stool and

hand stripped the last bit of milk out into a pail. A posse of calico-and-gray barn cats shadowed him because he played a game with them. He would strip out a small stream of milk and aim it at them, and they would dance around trying to catch it in their mouths. He would keep raising the stream until they were standing on their hind legs, and, finally, one of them would fall on its back. That ended the game and made Pop crinkle his blue eyes and chuckle.

He taught me how to strip the cows, but always kept an eye out for a sudden move by one of the big animals.

In the milk room, we poured the milk through gauze strainers into twenty quart cans we would carry across the yard to the dairy. Sometimes, milk was kept aside for feeding the calves we kept in Mr. Brewer's old barn.

After milking, we sat in the sunny kitchen at the round table covered with a blue-and-white oilcloth, dunked sweet rolls in our coffee, and listened to my father and my Uncle Carl getting things going in the dairy. I asked him one question after another: How do you grow coffee? Why does water freeze? How old is our elm? When will we mow the big field? He and my grandmother told people how I craved to know everything.

Everybody said my Uncle Carl was every inch a Swede: blonde, muscular, and quiet. He saved my life once when I was very little. I had a plastic pinwheel and broke it. My grandmother glued it, but said it would be lunchtime before it dried. Uncle Carl took me with him on the tractor to harrow a small field below the sheds. The wheel harrow sliced sharp metal disks deep into the plowed dirt to break it and make it ready for planting. I sat on the small battery box, facing rearward as we went back and forth towing the harrow across the field. When I thought it must be lunchtime and that my pinwheel must be mended, I decided to jump from the tractor and walk back. No doubt I would have fallen under the slicing steel wheels if Uncle Carl had not reached out with one hand and grabbed me in midair by the back of the shirt and hauled me back.

When I was thirteen, he saved me again, if not from death, from crushing injury. I was baling hay, driving the big tractor, hauling the baler down a slope in a corner of a field where morning glory vines had grown in thick with the hay. Even cut and raked, the whole corner remained damp and slippery. I felt the tractor slip a little to the left and made a small correction, but the force of the baler plunger drove the whole rig further off line. The baler had its own engine to power the giant plunger hamming away compressing the hay. Each of the two, big rear wheels on the Minneapolis Moline had its own set of brake and clutch pedals that, if you used them right, could help straighten out a skid or slide. I didn't yet have the skills, and over-corrected, pulling the tractor further to the left while the baler kept pounding straight ahead. Now, instead of the baler being behind me, it was coming up on my left side. With each powerful slam of the plunger, the whole rig started to lift off the ground and began to tip.

Uncle Carl had been across the field unhooking the windrow rake from the small tractor and saw what was happening. He ran hard down the slope, jumped up on the tow bar between the tractor and baler, and told me to jump off to the right. As I did, he slid into the seat and spun the steering wheel, setting the front wheels straight, and then worked the two brake pedals to slide the tractor so that it came into line with the baler.

Afterwards he told me how, sometimes, you had to have a feel of how the rig lined up. He said it was a seat-of-the-pants thing, and my young ass didn't have the feel yet.

. . . .

Uncle Carl, like many in those days, had contracted polio as a child. Perhaps it was a combination of his natural strength and his knowing how much he was needed for the work on the farm, but he recovered with only the slight tell-tale limp in the weakened leg which the disease often left. He was turned down for military service. My grandfather and grandmother made no secret about how that was fine with them.

My father was older than my uncle and ran the milk routes. A handsome man, his build and coloring were everyday, except for his eyes.

People talked about his hazel eyes changing color from brown to green to almost gold sometimes. He was the best fisherman around, neighbors all said. I can't remember the first time we went fishing any more than I can remember the first time I tied my own shoe. Sometimes, we went to buy grain over at Buck's Feed, and at one place, the road came alongside the slow spot on the river, a black mirror. We slowed down and went silent, both of us scouting for a ring breaking the glassy surface – a rising fish! Creeping the truck along like schemers, we smiled and watched the surface return to glass, hoping the fish would rise again. "We'll come back and get him," he would say. My father joined the navy soon after the war started.

. . . .

I loved the dark smell of a freshly plowed field. "*Ny jord*," Pop called it. It meant "new earth." But much as I liked to sniff the plowed dirt, plowing signaled the time to dig out the rock sled. It looked more like a big toboggan than a sled, and we stashed it in its own spot behind the tractor shed. One year, as I pushed through the cloudy cobwebs and kicked aside the jumble that had piled up since last year, I realized that I was performing a ritual. I performed dozens of little rituals on the farm, and over the years, I came to learn how rituals freight two emotions: The sameness of the routine provided me confidence and comfort, but as I grew older, I realized more and more that these small, familiar acts meant that another year had gone by as fast as turning a page in a book.

. . . .

Our farm, like most, sat laced with stone walls, but they weren't really for fencing anymore; we needed some place to put the year's new crop of stones. Farmers said that New England soil grew a fresh crop of rocks each winter. In the beginning, I needed Pop to help me crowbar some of the bigger rocks out of the ground and roll them onto the thick wooden sled, but I got stronger. One chilly spring day, Pop and I were pulling rocks when a black, spitting rain turned into a white, snapping sleet. The chain to the tractor had come loose, and I went to re-hook it. My hand slipped on the slick steel, and I pinched it good and hard.

Pop took off my glove to see, and told me to go up and let the Boss tend it. I didn't want to go and feel like a little kid, and I didn't want to leave Pop pulling rocks in the sleet by himself. "We're almost done," I said. He looked at me steady for a minute, wiped his forehead, and then handed me back my glove.

. . . .

HOME FRONT

. . . .

I remember two times that the police came out to our farm. Because our farm was on the state road and had a rail line going through it, the police said it could be a good place for deserters and draft dodgers to hide. We all kept our eyes open after that.

. . . .

I already knew most everything about loose haying and was learning—like we all were—about baling. If we set the baling twine to wrap too much hay, the bales got too heavy to lift; too loose, and they fell apart. Twine broke sometimes, but none of us liked using wire because it cut into our hands.

I tried to take on seed planting, cranking the shoulder-hung spreader, but Pop said, "By and by, when you grow up," which is what he always said when I nagged him to do things like drive the tractor. He took great pride in how well planted each field was. We put in alfalfa, timothy, clover, and of course we planted corn with a special machine. That first year with just the two us, we stood out and watched for the pointed green sprouts of corn to push up soon after Memorial Day, but only about half came.

"Tar," Pop said. "With the war I couldn't buy enough tar, and nobody had much left from last year. No tar coating and the damn crows got the seed."

That year, most farmers brought in an extra cutting of alfalfa to make up for the corn, but they couldn't count on that, so everyone agreed to pool what tar could be found. They would draw straws to see who got to plant and share corn next season and hoped they wouldn't need to do it again after that.

. . . .

We didn't have spare cash for me to buy the red-and-black war bond stamps sold every Wednesday at school. Some teachers had all the kids who brought in money stand so everybody could see who they were. I always wished I could stand up. When I told my mother, she said I helped the war effort plenty with my gardening and my grown-up farm work. The long letters we got from my father always had a place where he told me to help take care of the farm. In one letter, he retold me how he gave me my first job when I was little; how he had me stand with a stick in my hand at the top of the farmyard drive that led down to the state highway. My job was to wave the stick and keep the cows that were coming up from the pasture for milking from wandering out. He wrote about how he would tease me into making fierce faces and sounds at the cows to scare them back. He said I must have done a good job because not one cow ever got down to the highway.

One cold winter day we had no school bus, and Mr. Rawlings drove his daughter Laura and me in his ancient, half-ton Dodge. I knew Laura from school and from the time I went up to help Mr. Rawlings whitewash his milk shed. That day, she wore dungarees she kept hitching up, and was helping her pale mother strip and dry beans. She was nice to me during lunch. She gave me a rock she had painted to look like a frog. Afterward, she showed me how to play a game where we hit a ball on a rope to wrap it around a pole. She called it tetherball and I'm pretty sure she let me win.

For a time on our ride to school, Laura sat quiet, looking down at her scratched, metal lunchbox, and then just said out, "The German planes are going to come in the night." I asked her how she knew such a thing, and she said her uncle was an air raid warden and he knew it for sure.

Mr. Rawlings heard and he said in a steady voice, "We'll be OK. That's why you and Douglas pull down the blackout shades during the drills."

Some stores downtown, like Jennison Jewelers, put photographs of soldiers and sailors in their windows and kept the windows lighted all night unless there was a drill. Posters to join the service and to buy war bonds covered all the walls in the Prindeville Arcade. One poster that said

"Uncle Sam Needs You" pointed at people from everywhere. An Honor Roll monument now stood in front of Nevin's Hall, and the newspapers published the list of casualties every day.

At first, we kids didn't talk much about the war at school, perhaps because giving voice to our fears might grant them a toehold on our reality, but after a while, with news flashes on the radio, and war movies at the theater, we picked up on how real it was. Every day we pooled our eavesdropping, snooping and overheard talk. We watched adults for signs of fear. We knew they were trying to keep bad news from us. Sometimes, President Roosevelt came on the radio. I never heard him, but I heard Pop and the Boss talking about what they made of it. When I asked about the war, they always told me not to worry. I knew they didn't want me to be afraid. It worked out so that if the Boss thought I was getting afraid, she would have me go around the house with her and water her African violets and then sit with her and go through picture albums. The red- leather albums stored page after page of black felt paper pasted with shiny black-and-white pictures of the farm and our family. If one of our Guernseys became registered with the American Guernsey Association, she had Pop pose for a picture with it in front of the barn. I liked one picture of Pop and his four brothers, all in long, black coats and top hats, standing under our giant elm. I smiled to see him dressed like that instead of in overalls and boots.

The Boss always went to pick out the picture she took
of me with my first big fish.

She called it her favorite because the picture showed what I really looked like. She said how it looked like I'm watching real hard for something, like I know something is going to happen.

. . . .

The only thing I liked near as much as summer on our farm was Christmastime. I started scouting for any telltale signs right after Thanksgiving. I reckoned that the minute we started cutting out snowflakes in school, Christmas was in the stars. Every day in December, something pointed the way: a milk customer put a manger on his lawn; a store hung a "Merry Christmas" sign in a window; and our teacher had us draw cut-out Christmas trees to string around the room. We practiced carols for our recitals in the assembly hall and worked like clumsy whizzes on lamentable Christmas cards for our families. I lived convinced that everybody got swept up in the same Christmas spirit I felt.

Two weeks before Christmas, Miss Davis, our second-grade teacher, said how nice it would be if we could have a Christmas tree in our room. I shot up my hand and told her I could get one off our farm. She and the class got excited, and everyone told me how fine I was that I could do that.

Like many men in our town, my father came home on Christmas leave from the war. I ran off the school bus that day and told him what I had promised my class. He asked me how I planned to get a tree. I said I thought he would do it now that he was home. But he said no; I had made the promise, and so I would have to get the tree. He would truck it to school for me, though, he said. I took a bow saw and went out looking for a tree. In my eagerness to please Miss Davis and my schoolmates, I had chosen to ignore the simple truth that despite the great number of trees all around, only a few really looked anything like a Christmas tree, and most of those were pretty big. I chose the smallest one and set to sawing, but I couldn't get fixed under it right and just didn't own the strength to cut it down. I returned to the house with no tree. After supper, over pie and cheese, my father said he felt sorry about my predicament, but schoolrooms really didn't need Christmas trees anyway, in his opinion. After all, we kids were putting up class decorations day after day. He told how he never had a Christmas tree in his schoolroom. He said for sure that nobody would be mad at me. My grandparents and my mother nodded agreement all through his sum-up.

Before class the next day, I told Miss Davis I couldn't find a tree. She acted very kind about it and said that maybe that afternoon after school, I could look somewhere else on the farm. I said that I would, but I felt a sinking feeling. I felt sure I was heading deeper into shame and failure again because I thought for certain I wouldn't find a tree for the class. The bell rang for school to start, and I waited in dread for what would happen when Miss Davis told the class that I didn't get them a tree. But even before we sat down, the classroom door flew open. There stood my father. He walked in carrying a tree, a perfect Christmas tree in a fresh wooden stand. My father didn't say a word; he looked right at me and grinned as he set the tree down in the front of the room.

Miss Davis told the class to say "thank you" to Douglas's father. He tipped a salute and was gone, just like that.

I felt a rush of happiness, but there was something else. It confused me at first, and then I realized what it was: I felt safe, my father was home, and he had rescued me.

. . . .

Miss Davis said we were going to put on a pageant about how people in other countries celebrate their Christmases. She asked us if we had anybody in our families who came

from another country who could tell us about Christmas there. Lots of hands went up, but none faster than mine. She called on me with a smile. I said I could tell everything about Sweden because my Great Grandmother Peterson came to our farm every year at Christmas, and we did all the Swedish Christmas things.

Grammie Peterson, a tiny, gnarled old woman, wore her gray hair pinched back in a bun. With her bony face, walnut colored skin, and small, squinty eyes, she looked like the drawings we had of "tomten," the secret Swedish gnomes who help farmers and who bring presents at Christmas.

Everyone on the farm made a fuss over Grammie Peterson because she was so old.

The Boss always took photos of her, Pop, my father, and me to capture the four generations together.

On one Christmas visit, when I was an infant, Grammie Peterson bundled me into a white, wooden cradle every afternoon and sat with me outside to nap in the cold December air. My mother feared I would catch cold, but Grammie Peterson said how all Swedish babies nap outside and never catch colds.

For the pageant, I told the class all about how, in Sweden at Christmas, people would spread grain for the animals on a hay-covered plank. I told how families ate *lutfisk* and drank a wine full of nuts and fruit called *gloog*. I told them how *tomte* was like our Santa Claus. Talking to the class, I imagined being in Sweden for Christmas – deep, dark, green woods, all white with snow and animals feeding at our door.

My grandfather's sister, Moster Olga, also came to the farm every Christmas. Her task was butchering the pig we hung up over a tub in the tractor shed. She would skin and carve away all morning, filling brine barrels with pieces and making blood sausage in the afternoon. It was an old joke, but we always said the only thing Moster Olga left of the pig was its squeal.

My grandfather and I had our own Christmas decorating jobs— stringing colored lights around the porch pillars, hanging greens on all the doors, and draping red ribbon over the

"Hillcrest Farm" sign near the state road. One year, I wanted to build a manger near the cows out in the barn. I wanted to make the three wise men and the Baby Jesus out of cardboard, but Pop wasn't very religious, and he found lots of other work to keep getting in the way.

My mother and the Boss teamed up to set white lights in all the farmhouse windows and decorated the biggest tree we could fit into our living room. The ornaments were very old and delicate. One year, they tried some new lights that bubbled, but the lights cracked and dripped sticky syrup. I couldn't wait to start my nightly job of lighting the pine spice candles that we set up in every room. "It smells like Christmas," I told everyone over and over. When my mother read *The Night before Christmas* to me, I closed my eyes and imagined the whole story happening right there at the farmhouse.

Our milk route drivers especially liked Christmas time because customers left them tips or gifts out along with their empty bottles. The drivers told each other who had been generous and who had been cheap. On the farm, the celebration stretched from mid-December to New Year's. Over those days, family, hired hands, neighbor farmers, and friends all crowded in and out of our big kitchen, sometimes to get warm, sometimes to talk and sip *gloog*, and sometimes to snatch some of Moster Olga's *drommar* dream cookies. She pretended to scold them. They always said, "Olga, you need to put weights on these cookies. They're so light they float away all by themselves,"

She knew I liked *klenat*, the twisted fried donuts, hot out of the oil, so she would catch me when no one else was in the kitchen and have me scoop them out with a wire ladle and spread them on cheesecloth. She wanted me to have the first ones piping hot and crisp.

Every year at Christmas, the Boss picked a day to proclaim as "pie day," when everything we ate had to be in a pie. We started the first year with egg pie for breakfast and started adding new pies each year – from pork pie and potato pie to hamburger pie and fish pie. We would throw in whatever vegetables we had: carrot, squash, tomato, and pumpkin. We always ended supper with hot apple pie under a slice of salty cheese.

In my memory, I don't think of any single special Christmas when this happened or that happened. All those celebrations on the farm live within me;

folded, creased, faded and run together where I can't sort out one from another. I can't beckon them anytime I want. The memories arrive on their own, usually on a draft of balsam-scented air, or a few notes of a Christmas carol, or a somehow familiar pose of colored lights against snow.

When I sense the promise of those memories, I shelve whatever I'm doing. I can tell when it's time. It's as though I'm seated at a play, and I don't want to miss a minute of it. I close my eyes and the houselights of everyday life dim. Slowly, the stage comes to light inside the farmhouse. A warm flickering glow, brightly wrapped presents strewn around a lighted tree, and a cascade of laughing voices bring the stage to life. I hear carols. I smell balsam pine and wood smoke. I feel giddy anticipation. And I see them; all those from my life back then, there, coming out from the wings, smiling at me, reaching out to me. I'm there with them, happy and safe, sheltered by people who love me.

....

They called my grandmother "the Boss" for good reason; she seldom left the farmyard, but very little went on without her OK. She didn't act like the boss of all the work; she just bossed all of us who did the work. She knew how much could get done in a day and made sure it got done. She allowed for no chipped boards or faded paint on any building. Drivers could never sport tattered uniforms. When seasons changed, she told when we should stock wood and coal in the fall, or when we should muck out under the barn in the late winter. She bossed what day the farm got winterized and when it got changed back. If customers got behind, she got on my father to go collect. She used her strong, down-Maine voice to argue price with Simon, who bought our bull calves. She made me tell her every time I headed for the river and rang the barn bell at least once while I was gone.

Every room in the big farmhouse that admitted light also boarded her African violets that she set on delicate glass or silver plates. Pop said she finished first in her nursing class. She read two or three books a week and ate as many boxes of cream-centered chocolates. She loved Kate Smith's singing. Pop said that was so because they looked enough alike to be sisters.

All of us got a bundle of pleasure every time her mother, Great Gramma Hodgkins, came from Bar Harbor toting bags of cotton batting to visit and make crazy quilts. Pop and I would set up the wooden quilting frame in the dining room, and the two of them would set to cutting and sewing and building their quilts. Our pleasure came from listening to the Boss herself being bossed around by Great Gramma Hodgkins. I think Uncle

Carl liked it best because he was the one of us who got bossed the most.

I liked when Great Gramma Hodgkins came because she brought me copper toys. My Great Grampa Hodgkins outfitted houses and farms with lightning rods, and he made things for me from the copper he used. My favorite toy was a little boy with a fishing pole, and you could move the boy's arm back and forth. He had scratched "Douglas" on the back. We all knew the Boss would be extra grouchy the day Great Gramma Hodgkins went back to Maine.

One of Great Gramma Hodgkins's visits became a legend. She was ninety, and Uncle Carl had persuaded her to try an airplane ride down from Maine. We met her at Logan Airport outside, at the foot of the airplane stair ramp. Great Gramma Hodgkins' sturdy, square frame appeared at the top of the ramp in the clutches of a smiling, gray-uniformed stewardess who guided her down as though she was a frail two-year-old. Another stewardess followed carrying Gramma's floral carpetbag. At the foot of the ramp, Gramma shook off the fawning stewardess, walked straight to Uncle Carl, and shaking her fist at the DC-3, bellowed out, "Carl, you'll never get me on another one of those goddamned things as long as I live!" The stewardesses and the other deplaning passengers, who had been caught up in watching Gramma, gasped. Uncle Carl told me to quick grab the carpetbag so that we could hustle her off to the car. I sat in the back on the ride home and listened to her scold Uncle Carl for most of the trip.

"Carl, that damned airplane went this way." She flung a hand way up. "Then it went that way." She slapped it back down. "I'm going back to taking the bus. Either that or you can just come down to Bar Harbor and collect me."

I sat quiet as a mouse during the ride, zipping my fingernails silently back and forth over the woolen cord seats, and grinning as I watched her set her jaw hard and turn her head to glare out the side window.

. . . .

I knew and remember three of my great grandparents: The Boss's mother and father and Pop's mother. I spent time with Great Grampa and Gram-

ma Hodgkins in Maine. Great Grammie Peterson visited with us every Christmas. I knew Pop's four brothers and his sisters. Both the Boss and Pop talked easily about their families. One day, I asked them how they met and married. They replied in flat, dispositive unison that they didn't talk about that. I'm sorry I didn't have the courage or interest to ask again.

. . . .

Older kids—boys—took up playing at war on the playground and on rowdy walks home from the movies. Mostly they used their hands as guns or else spread their arms wide and made airplane sounds as they ran shouting, "Bombs away!" Boys drew pictures on their book covers of tanks and planes firing their guns. They talked about the afternoon radio shows like *Jack Armstrong* or *Dick Tracy* where they chased spies and you could get a secret decoder ring. I wished I could get a decoder ring but that was my chore time and I didn't get to listen very often. Bruce Person in my class said the rings were a gyp because the secret messages just said, "buy Ovaltine."

One day, it went all around school that Thomas Eckland, a boy in the fourth grade, had seen a German submarine out at the Cape. I ran out at recess, joining a knot of kids all around Thomas. They were piling questions on him about what it looked like, did it have a swastika? Did he see German sailors? Thomas' answers weren't satisfying the crowd. Finally he admitted that he hadn't actually been the one who saw it, but he knew the boy who did.

In school, we sang "My Country 'tis of Thee," but now we sang all the verses, all the way to verse four:

Our fathers' God to Thee,
Author of liberty,
To Thee we sing.

HOME FRONT

Long may our land be bright,
With freedom's holy light,
Protect us by Thy might,
Great God our King.

We held Victory Assemblies where some officials would come and tell us how important it was to work together, to pitch in, and to collect papers and save scrap and do other patriotic things.

We and sang "America the Beautiful" and even songs like "Over There" from World War I, and some extra hymns. We wrote letters on thin "V" mail paper to soldiers and sailors, sometimes to relatives and sometimes to strangers.

The letters were mostly the same: "I hope you are OK. All of us think about you and pray for you. God bless you."

We got letters and cards back from them. My favorite was a picture of Santa driving a Jeep full of presents. Our teachers, when they learned that someone's father had gone off to war, asked the rest of us to say a prayer. One day, we were told that Margaret James's father had been killed when his ship sank. She stayed out of school for a long time, and when she came back, no one knew what to do or say. If a kid was absent for a few days, we might wonder about it, but no one would ask.

For a couple of months during the war, we had a boy live with us on the farm. He stayed very quiet and mostly played inside with puzzles. He didn't know anything about farming. His mother had moved away to be near his father's base, but his father was sent overseas, and she came back and got the boy. His name was Eric.

. . . .

My mother's family lived in town, and I had three cousins—Dick, John, and Ronny— who were around my age. They liked to come out to the farm and sleep on the hay in the barn, which Pop and I thought was funny. I liked visiting them in town because I got to drink a tonic called Moxie. My Aunts liked it and kept plenty around but my cousins wouldn't touch the stuff because it was too bitter. I didn't get to drink tonic on the farm, so bitter or not I swigged it down. Visiting my cousins was exciting. One time a troop train of soldiers came through town and we ran alongside, down Waverly Street as long as we could keep up. The soldiers waved and laughed at us. One soldier threw some coins out but they landed in the tracks. Once, outside the cobbler shop, I heard men telling gruesome stories of what the Germans and Japs did to our boys. One of my cousin's friends said there were secret German spies all around. They asked me if I wanted to go see Tony Vilardi who got wounded in Africa, but I said no. When I got back to the farm, my grandmother scolded my mother some for letting me hear all that.

We had a lot of excitement in my town when the army decided to build a hospital for the boys coming home wounded. What made it so exciting was that we heard POWs were being used to build it, and if you went by, you could see them! By now I could ride my bike downtown, and I went to talk my cousins into going to see for ourselves. When we got there we found the building site was all wire-fenced in, but we could see dirt roads, skeletons of buildings, piles of red bricks, and stacks of lumber. Army trucks were grinding around, and we could see workers, but they were too far away to see what they looked like. At the chain-link gate, we came upon a young soldier in a khaki uniform with a white helmet and an MP armband. The guard smiled at us when we pedaled up. Dick, the boldest of us, rode up close and asked, "We heard there are POWs here. Is that right?"

The MP looked us over and nodded yes. We stayed silent waiting, three abreast on our bikes, for more, and finally, he shrugged and said, "We have some Italian prisoners. They come down from Fort Devens and do mason work on the new chapel."

"Can we see them?" Dick asked.

"No. And anyway, the chapel is way back there so they can't bother anybody."

"What are they like? Do they look mean?" we all asked.

"No," the MP said. "They just look sad."

. . . .

After a while, I began to think that the war would go on forever. More soldiers kept coming home wounded and worse. Striking on the milk routes, I would see a new gold star in some family's window. At the Hollis Theater, they showed war movies now, sometimes two, and a short feature where movie stars told you to buy war bonds. The most unsettling segments of the *Paramount News* was when they showed masses, thousands, of invincible looking goose-stepping Nazi soldiers. In *Life* magazine, with the bright red block on the cover, I could see pictures of a bombed-out Europe from right there in the farm kitchen. The brown radio with the green tuning eye on the kitchen shelf crackled at night, and Pop said we were hearing Edward R. Murrow and the real war in London.

I worried about my father and my uncles and all the men fighting so far away.

. . . .

One day when I came back from striking on the routes I saw two young women clearing brush that had tangled up on our long stone wall that ran beside Brewer Road. They were dressed in cut off pants and had their blouses untucked and tied in knots across their middles. They wore red kerchiefs.

"Who are they?" I asked the Boss.

"Farmeretts," she said. "Roosevelt has something called the Women's Land Army for America and they get girls, college girls it seems, to volunteer to help on farms. They'll stay for a week or two to do some big chore or help catch up on things that have gotten behind, then move on."

With my father gone, my mother moved into town to give a room to the girls. Carol and Donna were hard-and very quiet- workers. They seemed to talk to each other well enough, but when I tried to get some talking going they gave me one or two word answers and kept their eyes on their work. Uncle Carl saw my attempts and said, "They're too old for you, Douglas."

The night they left, the Boss said how the whole thing was kind of a wash. "We got the stone walls cleared, but the two of them ate like a crew of loggers."

....

One day old Mr. Brewer called and said that the Department of Agriculture people were coming to town and wanted to meet with local farmers. They had asked him to call around and get people to come. The meeting was to be a dinner meeting where they would talk about increasing production. "A dinner meeting at the Abner Wheeler House," the Boss speculated. "Must be important."

When the Boss, Pop, and Uncle Carl walked into the Abner Wheeler House they began to seat themselves among our neighbor farmers but were told by a man in a black suit that they were to sit at another, small table. There seemed to be no reason for it, but they went along, grousing among themselves about being separated from their friends.

Then the time came for the man from the Department of Agriculture to give his talk. He waited until all the squirming stopped and began. "I want everyone in the room to look over at this table. You all recognize the Petersons from Hillcrest Farm, I know. What they don't know is that they have won the Department's 'A' award for productivity." With that he walked to their table and handed Pop a certificate signed by Mr. Henry Wallace, the Secretary of Agriculture, and gave Uncle Carl a big red flag with a giant blue 'A' on it. Everyone stood and applauded, happy that they had managed to pull off such a fine surprise. It was left to Uncle Carl to say something, but true to his nature he just nodded and said, "Thanks."

The Boss thought the flag too showy to fly, so it got folded and put away.

....

For a while, in the third grade, a student teacher from the Normal School came to our class. Her name was Miss Hunter. She wore a blue apron and was very pretty; even Laura said so. I felt sure she liked me because she always called on me first if I raised my hand. Sometimes she would keep me after class and ask me questions about the farm or what I wanted to be when I grew up. I told her I wanted to be a navy pilot and fly off of aircraft carriers, like I told everybody else.

"Would you like to learn how to fly?" she asked.

I said, "Sure, but I have to wait and grow up."

She smiled and said, "Maybe."

Then one day, she came to class and set a wooden ladder back chair in the front of the room and rigged it up with a broom handle, wires, and some pedals on the floor. She called me up to sit in it and showed me how it all worked, just like a plane. It seemed easy and she called me a natural. I wanted to stay in the chair and keep flying, but she said other kids needed to have a chance.

After the Christmas holiday, Miss Hunter didn't come anymore. Miss Marshall, our regular teacher, said that Miss Hunter went to help with the war but I never knew what that meant. *Years later, on my first training flight at Pensacola, I remembered everything Miss Hunter taught me.*

All the kids I knew felt small. The war towered over everybody and everything we did. Big battles raged all over the world with big tanks and battleships, and people talked about big generals and admirals. The death of President Roosevelt shook the whole country, while we kids, with no agency of our own, just watched and waited for the end of the war.

PART TWO

GETTING BACK TO NORMAL

War's end brought more than euphoria; it brought the return of our boys and the return of full store shelves. Pent-up demand, not only from the war, but from the Depression, powered growth. The GI Bill and VA loans made it possible for the country to give birth to our "middle class." New developments, with their bright wood houses, popped up like weeds. War factories reconverted back to make cars, and others came on line to make the new refrigerators, automatic washing machines, and televisions. With the rest of the world in ruins, America was booming.

Adjusting to the country free from war was not without its own disruptions. Unrestrained, many free from shortage and want for the first time, Americans were exploring their new lives and exploration freights risks.

. . . .

In 1944, I could hear that the end of the war was starting to come on slowly. After D Day in June, when Pop and I worked, we talked quietly about how many more cuttings it would be before it ended. I said I hoped it would end before Big Red had her calf, but it didn't.

More and more, I heard adults talking about what was going to happen "after the war," especially after VE Day. That happened in May, then, during the day of August 14th, 1945, the Boss hurried out to find us and tell us that bulletins were coming over the radio. She said that we had dropped an atomic bomb on Tokyo, and that Japan sounded ready to surrender. During supper, the announcer on the radio said it was official: Japan had surrendered, and the war was truly over!

"Don Crawford at the ESSO station called and said he'll pump gas for anyone going to the victory party downtown," my mother announced. The Boss and Pop stayed behind while my mother drove us down to the spur-of-the-moment parade. Not far out of town, we began to form a loose caravan with other packed cars and trucks. I saw all five of the Swenson boys standing up on the back of their flatbed hay truck, shouting and waving, and I saw Mr. Rawlings and Laura in his old Dodge.

We wound all around the crowded downtown on Concord Street, blowing our horn and joining in with the shouting. I had never heard such a noise, or seen so many people waving flags. People set off fireworks. A bunch of boys and girls I didn't even know jumped in the back of our truck and, all laughing, we became part of the turmoil for a while. We found a place to pull over and got out to join the crowd of people snaking around in a line in front of the Memorial Building, some banging on pots and pans. It was hot as blazes but no one complained. We hugged everybody and they hugged us.

My cousins told me that the next day they went and witnessed a kind of real parade, a ramble of cops and firemen, air raid wardens and clubmen, and smiling, shirt-sleeved men who worked in the town hall building. The band was a dog's breakfast of assorted old men, high school kids in blue and gold uniforms, and women from the Catholic Eagles wearing green jackets, tall hats, and playing horns. They saw some war veterans. No more than a few dozen had made it home by that time, and half of those were banged up one way or another—limping, staring at things the crowd would never see.

All the farmers' families got together at Brewer's that night and put their problems aside. Everybody got dressed up—women in bright colors and men in dress shirts, excited, talking all at once mostly about what was going to happen now, how we were going to get back to normal. I felt it was so different from last time we met here. I saw some drinking and lots of laughing. Pop turned toward the wall a couple times and poured some whiskey into a paper cup. He always held that he didn't drink, but when he and I would go into the cold pantry for some afternoon hard tack and salted lard, he would take a sip from a brown bottle. "A nip," he would call it and put two fingers to his lips to show me I shouldn't tell.

Almost all the talking was about what everybody thought would happen now. Mr. Brewer said he thought he might sell some of his hay fields and make money because the boys coming home would need houses, but that he would keep his orchards on a slope behind our farm.

On a Saturday right after the war, I joined with a pack of kids downtown who were roving from one house to another to look at the treasures some of the boys brought back from the war. I touched a real German Luger and saw white Japanese flags with red markings, and some grainy, gruesome pictures, among other things.

HOME FRONT

When I rode my bike back home up into the farmyard it was almost dark. A man was standing in front of the dairy. I looked real hard and saw my father in his blue uniform, with his arms outstretched.

. . . .

For days, everything jumbled around. First, everyone would laugh and talk and grab my father to show him one thing and another and then it would get so quiet that I would clap my hands just to hear a sound and be sure everything was real. It could happen that all at once the whole farm-yard would be full of cars and trucks—Mr. and Mrs. Rawlings with Laura, the Swensons in two trucks, old Walter Brewer, the other farmers, even some men in suits who I didn't know. People brought things and stayed a while, and some just shook my father's hand and went on their way.

On a Sunday, my mother's family from downtown all came out. I had to take my cousins out to the barn so they could reach in the stalls and pet the cows. Over one or two summers I had managed to fool each of my cousins with a trick farm boys always pull on town kids. One edge of our biggest pasture ran a finger of good grass alongside the river. The only way to close the water off from the cows took using an electric fence. We could rig one up simple and fast. It took nothing more than one of our truck batteries, two lines of galvanized wire, porcelain glass insulators on each stake post and a special box to make the electricity pulse. The fence was easy to turn on and off and simple to drop a section or two if we needed to get a piece of machinery in.

My trick on my cousins was simple, too. I'd set us off to go fishing in a good spot I said I knew that lay beyond the fence. When we got to the fence I'd take hold of our two fishing rods and ask them to step down on the bottom wire and lift the top wire so I could slip in between. The shock they got hardly hurt them, but it always got me roughed up some as my cousins were all bigger than I was.

That first summer, my mother and father spent the evenings after sup-per sitting in two chairs they set up close together on the slope of the lawn looking toward the river and the valley. I watched the two of them from my room upstairs. Sometimes they stayed out in their chairs until it got dark and the fireflies swarmed thick over the hay fields as far as you could see.

It was a happy time. My father bought me a new rod, and we fished the "evening hatch" when mayflies and caddis flies would hatch on the water and fish would rise for them. He was still a real good fisherman. We picked a spot where our meadow stream ran into the river at a sharp angle that created a point of land. When the stream flowed fast, as it often did, it created a strong swirl hole where it hit the river. "Hydraulics," my father explained. "On a big river they can suck you right under."

Once we got settled in, I could see him working up to talk to me. Always a quiet man, now he was even more so. "Tell me how it was when I was gone," he began.

I didn't know how to answer so I shrugged and said "It was OK, I guess."

"Were you able to handle the work?"

I told him about the meeting at Mr. Brewer's and how we shared some equipment and divided up work where we could. Mostly I told him how everybody was so busy all the time with the war stuff like rationing and saving things and how everything was about making do and asking, "Don't you know there's a war on?".

"How did your mother fair?"

"At first she was pretty nervous, but the Boss kept her busy and she helped out with her sisters in town. She pitched in on some chores, but you know she's not a farmer." He smiled at that. We had a flurry of

catching fish for a bit, and when it slacked off I asked, "What did you see in the war?"

I didn't see the war so much as I heard it, "he said. They trained me down in Casco Bay to be a radio operator. I spent most of my time in a small room on a ship listening to signals and copying everything down. My friend Buddy was the one who sent out the signals. We were supposed to be three of us, but the Navy didn't have enough radio operators. We kept being put on different ships that needed us, so I stayed at sea most of the time going back and forth around England and Italy and France. I guess we got close enough in the war because a few times we heard huge thumps and the ship would swerve real sharp and scatter all our stuff."

He sat quiet for a while then said, "I guess there's not much more to tell except I never want to be closed in a small room or see the ocean again." He turned a smile on me and we fixed back on our fishing.

. . . .

With my father newly back home, I needed to be his striker delivering milk. He bought stiff, gray-and-white coveralls and a hat with a black bill. I had to show him the routes and all the changes, but he caught on fast. We picked up our old routine of stopping at Farley's Diner for pumpkin pie. On the first days he drove the routes, people came out and said, "Harry! It's good to see you home!" When we started haying, I stayed back and worked with Pop. I felt things were getting back to normal, like everyone said they would.

. . . .

Over the summer and fall the boys kept coming home from overseas. We could see them out on the state road hitchhiking. They always seemed to get picked up in short order. We could offer them rides, but we only went short distances for farm errands. At the Hollis Theater, newsreels showed sailors and soldiers streaming down the gangways of ships, pouring into milling crowds. When we went into downtown Framingham we saw lots of the boys wearing their uniforms, proud of what they had done. We kids always saluted them and they would smile and salute back. My father never wore his uniform, but he did have a small pin he called the ruptured duck. Sometimes he wore it on his milkman's overalls. It showed he was a veteran.

That year our school put on a special Christmas pageant and invited our relatives who had been in the service to attend. Every seat in the assembly hall was full, and people lined the wooden paneled walls. My father was delivering milk that day, but he stopped in for a few minutes in his milkman's uniform. We waved at each other.

On a very cold day just before Christmas, I was striking with my father on his long route that went into Southboro. With the war over, customers were in a happy mood and were being extra generous. My father told me to rattle the bottles and make a little noise when I delivered the milk, just to remind the customers who may have forgotten, that it was time to wish us Merry Christmas and give us a little gift. But at two houses he told me to be extra quiet. These were the homes of families that had lost someone and whose Christmas would be very painful.

. . . .

We had no close neighbors on the farm. We were five miles west of town on State Route 9, which some people called the Boston – Worcester turnpike and some called Worcester Road. Our official address read 1677 Worcester Road. Don Crawford's two-pump ESSO, under a red-and-white oval sign and fronted with a red Coca Cola ice chest, sat far across the road. The next-nearest thing was a small collection of houses, a post office, and an ice cream stand, called Fayville, a few miles west. We owned

nearly two hundred acres and rented three scattered hay fields from farmers who gave up haying, and we rented Walter Brewer's barn and his land next to us when he stopped dairy farming.

Hillcrest Farm sat atop a rise on the north side of Route 9. One arc of our crescent drive led up from the road, through tall lilac trees with shaded violets at their feet, into the large, crushed gravel farmyard. The other arc dropped back down to Route 9. On the other side of Route 9, opposite our upper driveway, was Gates Street, a small, nearly hidden road, which quickly bent left under thick trees and disappeared east back toward town. One special tree on Gates Street attracted lots of attention. Time after time, people pulled up into our farmyard and asked, "How do we get to the Gates Elm?" Early on in school, we all learned that the Gates Elm had been planted at the time of the Revolution and measured fifty feet around. Some said it was the oldest elm in the country. Why people would come all the way here to look at an old tree was one more thing I didn't understand.

(Many years later, I've learned that the Gates Elm fell victim to water table changes caused by the construction of the Massachusetts Turnpike.)

Our white farmhouse, with its four pillars, faced down to Route 9 across a sloping lawn shaded by three, tall horse chestnut trees. The trees blossomed with broad clusters of white flowers and produced chestnuts cased in shells with short, sharp spikes. I heard in a song about "chestnuts roasting on an open fire," and because I often ate the butternuts that grew on the trees along the dirt road to the river, I wouldn't accept the Boss's warning that horse chestnuts were inedible. I tried roasting a few of the bitter kernels on my own and learned she was right. The Boss explained that the chestnuts in the song were different chestnuts and that I could save myself trouble if I paid attention when she told me things.

The farmhouse welcomed light from dozens of tall "two-over-one" windows, even at the ends of the third-floor attic. Downstairs held a big farm-style kitchen, a dining room, a living room, two bedrooms, and a bath.

Upstairs had a smaller kitchen, four bedrooms, a sitting room, and a bath. Both the attic and the basement were full scale, walk-about spaces, a good portion filled half the year with mammoth storm windows and half the year with screens. A wood- and coal-burning furnace afforded hot air heat for the whole house. Brick fireplaces added heat to the downstairs living room and bedroom and to the upstairs sitting room on extra-cold evenings.

The blue-gray barn and silo sat across the oval-shaped farmyard. The large doors at one end of the barn faced the cement-block dairy building that framed the east side of the yard. Behind the dairy, we had a seven-stall garage for our milk trucks.

The side door of the barn facing the house gave one entry for the cows when they came up from pasture. We kept a small holding area fenced, but the cows seldom gave us trouble as they calmly waited in line and went to their own stalls. Another entrance for the cows opened on the back side of the barn.

The yard right behind the barn fell away to open the underside of the building so we could drive our tractor underneath and bucket load out the manure we shoveled down from the gutters behind the cows. Farther behind the barn stood our sheds for tractors, rakes, the baler, the manure spreader, and other machines. All kinds of odd lumber, pumps, small engines, and spare parts crammed the corners, and the dirt floor always smelled of gas and oil. To reach the sheds, we walked past a twenty-foot-wide covered, sunken, circular bin we called the sawdust bin, but it actually held wood shavings we threw under the cows for their comfort and cleanliness.

The most important structure behind the barn was the bull pen. It comprised a square blue-gray building with a door that hung suspended on a heavy rod and swung upward to open into a small, chopped up, dirt patch enclosed by rails of galvanized steel pipe. A huge, lumpy, wooden post, shiny and slightly tilted, stood in the center of the pen. Our brute of a bull often butted the door high open, charged out, and spent some minutes in the dirt pen, banging his horned head side to side on the post.

Behind the sheds, alongside the tractor road down to the hay fields and gravel pit, sat our pens and coops that sometimes had a congregation of pigs, goats, sheep, chickens, turkeys, and more, depending on what the Boss thought we should have.

Another rough path, grooved by our cows, led down from the barnyard between vine-covered stone walls and across the railroad tracks and into our pastures. The single-line railroad tracks ran east –west between two dense walls of wild grapevines. The only grapes I ever knew, before we had refrigeration in the stores, were the big, sweet-smelling Concord grapes that hung along those tracks in clusters as big as my two hands.

Our pastures stretched out from the gate at the railroad tracks, up along the side of our hill, and down into a bushy meadow, bordered at its far end by a tree-lined brook that ran into the reservoir. A day's pasturing for the cows had them feed along the slope, then toward the lower meadow and the brook, drink and rest in the shade, and then spend the afternoon grazing back to the railroad gate.

HOME FRONT

The pastures formed a rough elbow curving from right to left around two of our main hayfields, which connected to three more fields we used mostly for corn, through an ungated opening in the stone wall that marked them off. We could get to the cornfields from the state road, but sometimes we went through the opening in the stone wall and over a low stone bridge across the brook. The opening was barely large enough to fit through with the tractor and corn cutter-binder, and we all thought it best if my father or Uncle Carl did the driving. I never gave a thought to how much weight that small bridge carried.

My father told me that the nameless brook had a special origin: a deep spring in the side of a hill a couple of miles away. I put a sandwich in my knapsack, filled my new war surplus canteen with water, and Scratch and I set off to find that spring. We followed the brook upstream, back under the state road, across rough fields and through thick, prickly brush, and up a slope covered in huckleberry bushes. When we came to the end of the bushes, the hill flattened out like a bench seat and turned swampy. We spent an hour or so trying to find the edges of the swamp and a path to the spring. I finally figured that the spring lay somewhere out in the bottom of the swamp, and that Scratch and I really had found where our brook started. I felt proud of my first solo exploration.

The brook, always cool and full of bugs and crayfish, flowed, deep-shaded, through our lower pasture and under the small stone bridge where it made a hollow, echoing sound. I could idle alone for hours in the shade, lying on my belly or hunched on my knees peering into the water for a brown-green crayfish to show from under a rock. I learned that to catch one I had to have my hand in the water behind it and move, very slowly, close enough to where I could snatch it. They pinched sometimes but they didn't really hurt that much. If I caught one, I would sometimes run to where the brook flowed into the reservoir and toss the thing out and watch to see if a fish grabbed it. If I had my fishing rod with me, I would use the crayfish for bait.

And I almost always had my fishing rod with me. If I wasn't doing chores, or haying or in school, I was fishing. My father took me fishing before I can remember much else. I felt excitement the very first time I held a stick pole, watching for the line to pull tight, hoping for a fish to bite. Part of the excitement came from the expectation – it might happen or it might not—and I never knew which. Every time I drew near the water, I brimmed with hope, and each day felt like a brand new chance to be happy. For me, nothing felt more exciting than the shudder of a live, wild fish pulling against me. I spent my time on the water alone with my thoughts washed clean and reduced to one, simple, contented focus.

I capped my fishing days bringing my fish up to the farmyard for the Boss and my father to admire. I caught mostly perch, blue gills, and bass, but often enough, I caught ferocious-looking, sharp-toothed pickerel. Once in a while, when a rough squall blew in, I caught a special fish. If I saw dark clouds roiling up, I grabbed my rod and rushed to a rock-lined, narrow channel where, for no reason I could figure, I caught white perch. Silver scaled, with a dark back and a thin black line down the side, they looked like saltwater striped bass. They weren't much bigger than the other fish and didn't taste any better, but because I could catch them only among rocks, in a storm, and with extra effort, they became special. No one knew how white perch got into our reservoirs.

I considered the reservoirs, from the railroad trestle up to the dam near Laura's place, to be my home waters, my river. I knew every inch: the deep spots, the coves spotted with lily pads, the place to find long, black water snakes, the thick pine groves planted to shield the water, and the stretch where the water flowed big-river fast and cut a wide ox-bow in the meadow below the dam.

I knew the exact day when the new issue of *Field and Stream* magazine was in the library and, after a while, the librarians started holding it aside until I got there. I sat in the front reading room and read each issue from cover to cover including the ads for things like the sure-catch rubber worm and the plastic minnow that fish couldn't resist. Each cover of the magazine showed some spectacular scene of hunting or fishing. One cover showed a huge, wild- eyed largemouth bass, all contorted and leaping out of the water with a frog-like fishing lure hooked in the corner of its mouth. The story, like all of them, told in detail, how the author stalked and tricked the fish, which they always called "lunkers," this time in the Everglades of Florida. The cover story might be about muskellunge in Maine or marlin in Hawaii, but every one made me dream about someday going there and catching that fish. The one that made me dream the most told a cover story about fishing for rainbow trout on a ranch in Montana. I told the librarian that one day I was going to go to Montana and catch rainbow trout.

When I went to the library the next month, she went to her desk and brought me the old magazine to keep.

. . . .

I found more than places to dream about fishing in Field and Stream. I once found a tip that amused the Boss no end. It was a tip on how to catch night crawlers. The article went over the way most people catch night crawlers - by going out at night with a flashlight and plucking them off the lawn – but it told about a new way to catch them in the daytime. It said to mix a tablespoon of dry mustard in a quart of water, scrape off the top of a worm hole and pour some of the mix down the hole. I tried it and, sure enough, in a few seconds after pouring the stuff down, up came a night crawler shooting out to get away from the burning liquid.

Every time I asked the Boss for some dry mustard she hustled herself out to watch me and laughed in amazement as I filled a can with the big worms.

. . . .

I only saw the Boss get on to Uncle Carl but once. I came out of the barn hearing the Boss tearing into Uncle Carl who was standing in the farm yard with no pants on and a smudge of blood on his leg. Pop was behind him holding a rake at his back like a prod. "Go on, tell her," Pop said. Everyone who worked on farm machinery knew the rule that if you needed to work on a piece of equipment, you shut it off first. Uncle Carl, who knew he was the best machinery handler around, thought he could get away with unclogging the baler without shutting it off. He did get it unclogged, but the built up pressure caused the big plunger to spring down before he could get his leg all the way out of the chute. One of the forks on the plunger caught his pants and began to pull him into chute. Lucky for him, he was not wearing a belt and, over the course of one more plunge, the machine stripped off his pants and gave him a good wallop on the leg. He was strong enough to pull himself out his mix-up with the baler, but it was some time before he got out of his mix-up with the Boss.

. . . .

The veterans who hadn't married before going off to the service wasted no time when they got home. They may have suffered their own individual, personal ordeals during the terrible duration of the war, but they all had the same dream: a home and a family. They married, built their homes, and formed new families. Pop held that it had always been the only way to conquer war's death.

My mother's youngest brother, Alec, returned home from the navy and took a job right away with Framingham Welding, a company newly started by his friend, another returning sailor. Handsome, with dark hair, nicknamed "Blackie," Alec married his childhood girlfriend Margaret and built a small Cape Cod-style house they soon filled with five children.

Uncle Alec, Margaret, my mother, Uncle Faust

He, like so many others coming home, brimmed with exhilaration. The Depression had passed. The war had ended. Alec saw a safe and secure life ahead for himself, for Margaret, and for their children. He felt nothing was lost or ever would be.

His older brother, my Uncle Faust, tried to come back to civilian life but couldn't do it. He had served in the thick of the battles in the Pacific and had come to crave adventure. He harbored suspicion of our post-war elation. He felt everyone was too comfortable, that everything was just landing in our laps. He thought and said—sometimes too loudly—that things weren't right.

"You're all caught up buying chrome cars and television sets and you don't see what's coming." He argued that just because people went through the Depression and the war, they didn't automatically deserve a good life. He got himself into some small scrapes. None of us felt surprised when he reenlisted in the navy. Not long after he left us, the Korean War began.

. . . .

The milk business started to pick up, and it became hard for us to run the dairy longer and still keep up with the farming and the routes. With the war over, we thought we could find men to hire, but most of the boys coming back didn't much want any part of farm work. Some of them learned about the GI Bill that would send them to college so that they could get good jobs. A lot of them joined the fire department or the police department where jobs had sat open because of the war.

My father heard we could get help from the Lyman School for Boys, the reform school where all of us boys were told we would be sent if we misbehaved. I couldn't imagine having a boy from a place like that working on our farm. Pop and my mother posed against it, but the Boss said we needed the help. She said how we wouldn't be able to bring in enough hay, and we couldn't afford to buy any.

My father fixed up a place behind the boiler room, and the boy could use the bathroom that the dairymen used. The boy we got was named Charlie McPhail. He was sixteen and looked very tough even though he was sort of thin. He had a gray scar under his left eye and a reddish blotch on his throat. I heard that boys in the Lyman School were always fighting, and if you went there, you would be in fights and get beat up. I was afraid ever to go there. My father said he picked Charlie because he understood machinery and could fix cars and trucks, and it turned out, he could make almost anything run. I asked my father why Charlie was sent to Lyman School, and he said Charlie stole cars. He never kept them; he just took them and drove around for a while. But he always kept one hubcap.

Charlie fit right in to the work on the farm. Our New Holland hay baler sometimes snapped the hemp wrapping cord, and we had to stop everything right there in the field to fix it. I showed Charlie how one worn side pulled the whole thing off center, and he made a small block of wood to fix it. He was a good worker, I had to admit. He followed Pop around asking how we did this and that and what all needed to be done. I kept him at a distance for the first few days, but he acted friendly, and I was glad we were getting some help with things.

In September, the Boss said Charlie should go to school. Dick and Bob were back in the dairy, and we were catching up on work. Besides, school ended plenty early enough to leave time for things. I had him sit next to me on the bus and everyone stared. I liked that everyone could see me sitting next to such a tough boy from the Lyman School and that he was my friend.

Charlie felt funny because he was older than the others. The school wanted to see what grade he should be put in. Trouble started at recess that first day. Big Joe Riley, a bully with gray teeth and a mean face, came over to me and asked how I felt about having a real criminal living on our farm.

"You should be afraid that Lyman School guy will rob you or even murder you and run off."

I said Charlie wasn't a criminal and wouldn't do that. Joe laughed and pushed me in the chest and looked over at Charlie, who was watching us all along. Charlie walked steadily to us and didn't stop or put up his fists, but swung his left hand from down at his side. I heard the smash and saw blood run out of Joe's nose. Joe didn't fight back. He saw the blood and just walked through the circle of kids who had formed around us and went back into the school.

My grandfather came and picked Charlie up. He wasn't going to be able to come back to school even though I told everyone Charlie was just trying to keep Big Joe from hitting me.

Early next morning, when Pop and I went out to the barn to get ready for milking, I saw something shiny near the boiler room. It was a hubcap. Pop shook his head and said, "Charlie took a souvenir from somebody's car."

....

With my father home, the work divvied up pretty much by itself. Uncle Carl, the best one to do the work when it took driving the tractor, could always get the most hay cut and baled off a piece of land, everybody said. In his morning work, he got the dairy up to steam and helped my father load up the milk drivers. My father ran the milk routes. He figured out how much milk we needed every day; how many quarts of regular, how many skim. We sold half pints of light cream and heavy cream. In the summer, we sold chocolate and strawberry milk, and we sold egg nog in the winter. We sold raw milk, but Pop always tried to talk people out of it if they came by in person. He told them, and our route drivers, that raw milk carried bad bugs. To make his point, he would show them one of the gauze strainers we poured the fresh milk through, always flecked with blood and solid bits. A man from United Fruit Company came by one day and asked if we would be interested in buying some Melzo, a mix to make banana milk. We mixed up some, and it didn't taste good.

Wednesday was collection day, and if customers were late two weeks, my father had to go back and call on them. He also looked for new customers, especially in the new housing developments. If someone moved out of a house, he kept an eye out for the new people. He decided how many drivers we needed. He also liked to grow vegetables in a small plot near the road.

Pop and I looked after and milked the cows and did the fieldwork. Charlie acted as a chore hand for whatever else we needed. I had plenty of time to spend alone on the river, and I did.

The Boss took care of the books and the money, and once or twice a day, she came out into the yard and hollered out to Pop, Uncle Carl, or me something she wanted to be done. Whichever one of us she got hold of first got assigned to pick up any bit of paper or other trash that had blown into the farmyard.

My mother sort of helped the Boss. She did laundry, cranking the rollers and hanging the wash. Sometimes, she had to add "bluing" to make the sheets white. She canned corn and beans and whatever we had grown. Whenever one of the dairymen brought over a big cake of ice to the kitchen sink, she would chop it up with a pointed pick and layer it around our food in the ice box. She mopped and dusted a lot and made me clean windows with newspaper and vinegar.

. . . .

In the fall of 1947, Uncle Carl said we should go to the Eastern States Exhibition in Springfield. He had bought a used Jeep for a hundred dollars thinking we could use it as a small tractor, but it wasn't very powerful, sat too low, and you had to buy special parts to hook it up to plow or pull anything. He said he got his money's worth just bouncing it around in the pastures, but we needed a tractor. Besides, the "Big 'E'" had been closed during the war, and he said we should all go to the reopening.

Mr. Rawlings and Laura went with us. We hit the fall weather just right with a frost crunch in the morning and red, orange, and gold leaves against a perfect blue sky the rest of the day. The army and navy had taken over the "Big 'E'" for training during the war as part of the war effort, we understood. Now, people were so anxious to get "back to normal," as they called it, that the whole grassy fairground stood jammed

with people brushing shoulder to shoulder, wearing warm smiles to fellow strangers who all shared their relief and hope. A band far off played marching music, which was hard to hear over the jumbled noise of the crowd. Race cars warmed up, throwing dust and noise in the air.

After we had gone through the green-and-white National Dairy Show building, Uncle Carl and Mr. Rawlings went off to look at equipment. Laura and I wandered around the animal exhibits where we saw lots of 4H kids with their calves and goats and sheep. We followed our noses to the food stands. A bright, new Coca Cola sign announced Coke's return. Much of Coke and Pepsi "went to war," along with cigarettes and chewing gum, and we were left with a cola called Spur. It tasted like molasses.

"You and I should join 4H," Laura declared as we walked around. "But we'll compete with baking pies and cakes. I like cooking better than brushing shit out of some calf's tail."

"I will if you will," I said.

On the drive back, slowed down with traffic, Laura and I listened as Uncle Carl told Mr. Rawlings that he found a bigger Minneapolis Moline that we really needed now because we had to set up the small tractor for bucket loading and for running the ensilage blower. Mr. Rawlings said how everything he looked at was out of his reach.

"Maybe you buy on time," Uncle Carl said. "Minneapolis Moline let us buy our tractor and pay for it so much a month."

The milk business kept getting better, and we needed more hay. We had a funny shaped piece of shrubby land we wanted to use, but we had to clear it. As a first step, Pop and I set a plan to burn it off. We waited for a day with little wind and set the fires. We had no trouble walking the edges and keeping the smoky fire bounded using wet burlap bags, steel rakes, and shovels. The problem started for me the next day with some itching and scratching. By afternoon, I was near sick with itching and weeping blisters.

"Poison ivy. From the smoke," the Boss said. "Pop's immune and now you will be, too."

Pop stood off a ways in embarrassed silence, with his hands stuck deep down in his pockets. After she slathered me in calamine, and sent me off for new clothes, I could hear her out in the yard cornering Pop by the barn and giving him a real loud scolding. I wished I had known you could get poison ivy from smoke.

. . . .

One summer, old Mr. Brewer's grandson, Tommy, came to visit from Worcester. I was glad to have a boy my age so near to play with for the first time. I had a new red Radio Flyer wagon with lacquered wood slats on the sides that I proudly treated as my truck. Tommy and I used the wagon to haul stones, old bricks, and lumber scraps to a small depression out of sight from the road. We worked on building a hideout I had started weeks before. At the end of one day's work we said good-bye, and I started to pull my wagon toward the farm when Tommy said I should leave the wagon down in the depression. That way, he said, I wouldn't have to haul it all the way back to the farm today, and then pull it all the way back to our hideout tomorrow. He said how, if we covered it with some branches, no one could see it down there, so it would be safe.

When I got back to the farmyard, Charlie was working on the loose tailgate of the pickup. "Where's your wagon?" he asked.

"Tommy said I should hide it down in the gully under some bushes so I wouldn't have to pull it back and forth every day."

Charlie thought on it for a minute and then, putting his tools away, said, "We better go get that wagon. It's supposed to rain."

It was a short drive down Brewer Road, and when we stopped at the right spot, I jumped out and ran down into the depression to find my wagon gone. Charlie and I looked all around. "Show me where?" he asked me three times. Charlie threw around some branches and told me to get in the pickup. We stopped at Mr. Brewer's place and told him and Tommy what happened.

"What do you think could have happened?" Charlie asked.

"I can't imagine anyone stealing a kid's wagon," Mr. Brewer said.

My wagon sat back in the farmyard the next morning. Charlie came up behind me as I went to it and said, "Walter Brewer and I went back last night and found it. You must have been looking in the wrong place." I didn't think so, but I was just happy to have my wagon back.

When I went to find Tommy and tell him, he said that his grandfather was making him stay in their yard from now on because he feared Tommy could get lost out here in the country. I worked on my hideout alone.

. . . .

I didn't spend all my time on the farm. My mother's Italian family in town presented a ready and warm haven. My cousins Dick, John, and Ronny were slightly older than I was. Dick and John were brothers, but we all behaved more like brothers than cousins, even though I shifted in and out of their lives. Each of our mothers was noted for the special taste of her tomato sauce; my mother's, dark red and spicy; my Aunt Esther's, or-angey and rich; my Aunt Theresa's, rosy and very meaty. I regularly got to sample my aunts' sauces on Sundays because of my peculiar church going.

Religion was not a part of life on the farm; we said no prayers, attended no services. I sensed a presumption of God, but nothing more. Still, I needed to be sent to church, it seemed to me, as a way to "civilize me," who they saw as a rough piece of country work.

"I don't want your mother's people to think you're out here being raised by wolves," my father said.

The first church they tried out on me, a big windowed, tall-spired, white Congregational church, stood full of light shining off bright, maple wood. I mostly sat at a small table in the basement coloring in books, and singing simple songs. My father dropped me off and picked me up and never asked what went on or what I learned. They stopped sending me after a few weeks. In the fourth grade, I went to school with a girl, Phyllis Parmenter, whose father served as the priest at the Episcopal St. Andrews, and for a short time, spent hushed Sundays in the imposing stone church. The biggest thing that happened while I attended St. Andrews was that my Sunday school class was taken to a synagogue so that we could learn about a different religion. The service turned out to be a special one for the Rabbi's son, and lasted three hours.

Eventually, I could get to church on my own and satisfied everyone's felt responsibility for my religious exposure by attending St. Tarcisius, the Italian Catholic church where my cousins belonged. When church was over, I could pick which aunt (and which tomato sauce) I wanted to join for Sunday dinner.

My aunts and uncles treated me with casual tenderness. My cousins were all hard-working boys who never got into serious trouble. My cousin John had an extended paper route that took him all afternoon right to dinnertime to finish and also shined shoes on the weekends. Every once in a while, I would help John with his paper route. One day, when we went to the news company's shed to pick up the papers, all the paper boys stood crowded around the latest edition of the *Boston Herald* fresh off the truck. The huge headline told that Babe Ruth had died.

The Boss didn't worry about my being churched nearly as much as she worried about what I wore, especially on my feet. I had barn boots and dairy boots and winter boots, all of which came off before setting foot in the house. I needed the boots sometimes, but I really liked going barefoot.

It was easy and it seemed I should go barefoot so as to match what I was – a farm boy. The Boss lectured me over and over about stepping on a nail and getting lockjaw. I thought she was making that up because I talked too much. She said nurses knew about things like tetanus and bacteria and that it was no joke. To try to get me to wear shoes, she ordered a pair of Indian moccasins from L.L. Bean in Maine. I really liked the beads and leather tassels on them, but they weren't all that sturdy. I wore them out in no time, and we went back to arguing. Then one day the school called and the Boss announced, with a laugh, that our shoe battle was over: all the kids in school were to get a new vaccination for tetanus.

We kids were quiet as church mice on the bus ride to the big school in Boston where we would be getting the new shots. One boy asked our teacher who rode up front, "Will it hurt or make us sick?" She told all of us that it wouldn't harm us. When the boy asked how she knew that, she said it had been tried on the soldiers and sailors in the war and it worked fine.

Soon, I was driving the trucks and tractors almost every day and I didn't like driving barefoot. My mother bought me a new pair of rubber-soled gym shoes everybody called sneakers. She said that now with the war over, companies could get the rubber to make them. They were cheaper than leather shoes and with the way my feet were growing, sneakers were the right thing for me, she said. All the kids were wearing them, and I gave up going barefoot except for when I went fishing.

When the Boss got done worrying about my boots, she turned to fretting over what I wore. I had one blue denim coat with a corduroy collar that I was to wear outside and in the barn and nowhere else. I couldn't come into the house with it on and I absolutely couldn't wear it to school. Uncle Carl explained that one time when he was little he wore his barn coat to school and the kids made fun that he smelled like manure. He told the Boss and it upset her something awful.

The Boss and I agreed on one thing: Strap overalls didn't suit me. Even my mother said that when I wore them I looked like I was wearing a barrel hung on me with straps. We were all pleased when Sears started selling dungarees with front patch pockets held on with copper rivet fasteners. I thought I looked like a cowboy in them and the pockets held a lot.

. . . .

If I wasn't working or fishing, I joined my cousins for the Saturday matinee at the Hollis Theater downtown. We saw two features, usually one western and a war picture. Five cartoons ranked OK with us, but seven was better. The serials, though, were pretty poor. We could always spot where they changed something that allowed the hero, who was doomed last Saturday, to cheat death this Saturday. Dick, the oldest, did like the serial about *Nyoka the Jungle Girl*, though.

The whole thing began with some previews and a news reel that involved our participation. When the familiar concluding credits to the news reel rolled on screen, we kids always shouted along with each word: "The eyes and ears of the world. The End. Paramount News!" declaiming the start of the real show.

One Saturday, the Hollis showed a musical cartoon where we were supposed to sing along following a ball that bounced above the words to the song. All the kids booed so much that they never showed another one.

Tribal-like social order dominated our Saturday matinee. Kids came from neighborhoods such as Coburnville, the Junction, Saxonville, Tripoli, and the Center. Fuzzy rules set out who could cut line in front of whom under what circumstances. If a boy left the line for some reason, he had to point to the boy behind him and tell out loud to everyone, "He's saving my place!" If someone broke the rules, the kids involved hurled evidence at each other and those standing around shouted out who was right. By and large, boys and girls wanted to cluster with kids from their neighborhood so that, once inside, they could rush by the lobby posters announcing "Free Dishes Every Wednesday" to claim their usual seats.

Other than the endless arguments about who would win a fight between Roy Rogers and Gene Autry, I never saw any real rowdiness in line. I think that was so because any kid acting up could get scolded and cuffed behind the ear by an aunt or neighbor passing by, because any of them was empowered to enforce discipline.

A few kids from well-to-do neighborhoods got dropped off. The cacophony of us kids standing in line was brought down to a hush when a car pulled up. With no anger or envy, we figured that those kids probably had movie money given to them.

I don't remember why, but for me, my cousins, and most of my friends, movie money was our own responsibility. We weren't really poor, and it didn't cost that much, but for some reason we had to provide our own movie money. Some boys, like my cousin John, had paper routes, shined shoes, or stocked shelves, but for many of us, returning empty bottles was our source of cash. Small bottles cashed in for two cents and large ones for a nickel.

One boy, a bully I didn't like, used to steal bottles from the back of his own father's package store and try to get one of us to return them for cash and split the take. Very few boys would do it.

HOME FRONT

The magic number for me was twenty-six cents: twelve cents for the ticket, ten cents for the popcorn, and four cents for the Nibs licorice candy—if I bought it at Bond's Drug Store, not in the movie. So, on Saturday I rode my bike to town to meet up with my cousins, and we decided how much we needed. Often, we found enough by scouring for bottles around the streets or asking a nice neighbor for hers.

If we had trouble finding bottles on the streets, my cousin Dick and I would look in the railroad yards. While the days of "riding the rails" was pretty much over, we still had our hobo jungle where unfortunate men lived and where they drank Pickwick Ale. An empty of Pickwick Ale was worth a nickel to Dick and me, but it was also worth a nickel to its owner.

My cousin Dick, at thirteen, stood as big as some of our teachers, and I could run like the wind. Our plan held that we would walk along the edge of the tracks bordering the hobo jungle looking down to spot a bottle. My job was to slip down on the cinders, grab the bottle, and run, while his job was to fight off anybody who came after us. We did have one encounter. My cousin Dick told it that while I was reaching for a bottle, a hobo man rushed out of the brush, but Dick ran down and chased the man away. In truth, there *was* a man in the brush, but he was relieving himself, and he was too old to chase anybody. Even so, our one adventure caused kids in line to point us out to others for our daring.

One Saturday morning before we went to the movies, we went to see a boy who was in an iron lung because he had polio. We lined up in silence and walked through the house. He was in a quiet, front living room, and all I could see was his head lying on a pillow, sticking out from the round cylinder of a machine that made hissing sounds. He had dark hair, and I didn't know his name, but I said "hello" and he said "hello" back. His mother followed us out and called to us as we walked away, "It was very nice of you to come by."

People said you could get polio from the drinking fountain at the Hollis Theater or from swimming at Learned Pond or even from chewing a certain kind of bubble gum, but they always said that polio wasn't contagious.

I had never had so much as a cold and couldn't imagine what that boy must have been feeling. I became sad every time I thought about him lying there, trapped in that steel tube, not able to be outside.

. . . .

I took a bus to visit my Aunt Helen in Boston sometimes. She lived in a stone building with high ceilings on Beacon Hill. She was the oldest—and everyone said the most beautiful—of all my mother's sisters. She wore makeup all the time. Aunt Helen had been married to an important man once. He bought her a Packard car even though she could hardly drive. He got shot down in the war. She had no children of her own so, as my mother told me, she liked to borrow me once in a while to show her friends. I heard she borrowed my pretty cousin Debbie sometimes, too. When I visited, I stayed in a corner room lighted through tall, gauze-curtained windows and reached by way of a wooden door that, without a sound, slid out from inside the wall.

Aunt Helen sold perfume at a counter in a fine store called Bonwit Teller. She took me to concerts at night in Jordan Hall and once, while she was working, had a woman in a blue suit take me to a museum full of things from Egypt. We went to Nantasket Beach once, but Aunt Helen just sat on a bench holding up an umbrella like it was raining.

Aunt Helen guarded me closely. I was allowed to play on the front walk and in the small garden behind her building. A gate at the end of the garden opened onto a green belt of trees and grass that ran alongside the Charles River. One warm, sunny day, I saw lots of men fishing on the bank and had to find out what they were catching.

I spotted three old fishermen, sitting in beach chairs, talking back and forth to each other and made for them. They smiled when they saw me walk up.

"What are you catching?" I asked.

One of the men, wearing a crushed hat, said, "Mostly we're after yellow perch and carp."

I said I had never caught a carp.

One man, a black man with gray whiskers, said, "Come stand by me and we'll try to catch one."

I asked what he was using for bait, and he told me he used balls of dough mostly, but sometimes leftover pieces of meat.

"I like to use worms, but they're hard to come by in the city. You a fisherman?" he asked.

I told him about fishing on the farm. He said that sounded like fun and asked what I caught and what I used for bait. He showed a big interest in how I caught crawfish and used them. He called out to the other two men about it.

"George, William, this boy says he uses crawfish for bait and catches lots of fish."

William didn't seem sure what a crawfish was, so I went over and told how they were like tiny lobsters that lived in streams. I explained how you put the hook through the tail to use them. I was about to tell the men about my trick to catch night crawlers with dry mustard, when George yelled out and held up his fishing rod that now had a big bend in it. He landed a good-sized catfish. The four of us were bent around his pail, chatting our admiration, when I heard my name called out.

We all looked up to see my Aunt Helen tramping toward us. Once on us, she reached down and grabbed my hand and gave a jerk that pulled my arm straight to my shoulder. Without a word to the fishermen, we stormed back to Aunt Helen's place. Once inside, she gasped for breath and seated me on a hard chair.

"Douglas, it's dangerous for you to be down by the river talking with strangers. This is the city. You have no idea who those men are," she said. She didn't care when I told her that they were my friends and that they were just fishermen.

That night her friend, Tom, came by to take us to dinner. He was older than Aunt Helen and very handsome in a gray suit and red tie. As he came in to sit down, Aunt Helen told Tom about my hanging out with rough men down by the river. He smiled an easy smile and said he didn't think the old fishermen were anything to worry about. Then he turned away from Aunt Helen toward me and winked.

Aunt Helen fretted that I didn't have a jacket to wear to dinner, but Tom said a sweater would be fine. She made me put back my tan sweater and put on my blue one. She wet a comb and ran it through my hair.

The ride to dinner was the first time I had ever been in a taxi. The restaurant didn't have a sign outside, and I figured out, after a while, that it was a special club, and Tom was a member. We came into a hallway where I saw sculptures of women dancing. I could see several dining rooms where the walls were dark wood and hung with paintings of all sizes, each with its own small light. Mostly they were paintings of gardens and woods.

A man in a tuxedo led us into a round room, and I was taken right away by how glittering it was. Crystal chandeliers threw soft light down on white tables set with shining silver and sparkling glasses. Our table sat tucked around the dimmed edge of the room, leaving the small center to hold tables set with flowers and that waiters could use to fiddle with peoples' meals before they served them. It was all very quiet.

"What would like for dinner?" Tom asked me.

When I answered, "I like hot dogs," Aunt Helen whispered to me, "No, Douglas. You can have hot dogs back at the farm."

Tom smiled and asked if it would be OK if he ordered my dinner. He ordered lobster and I was proud to show him how the Boss had taught me the down Maine way to crack open and eat the things.

Lots of people came over to Tom to say hello and shake his hand. They were all dressed up and talked about things going on in Boston that I didn't understand, and they always snapped on big smiles when Tom introduced me. I had never been through such an evening or seen such sights.

The next morning, Aunt Helen handed me a small box and said it was a present from Tom. Inside I found a note and a baseball. The baseball was signed by every player on the Red Sox. The note said that next time I came to Boston, we would go to a game.

There was no next time with Tom. The next time I went to visit Aunt Helen on Beacon Hill, she had a new friend.

. . . .

I spent my seventh, eighth, and ninth grades trying to mix in with town kids at Lincoln Junior High School, which sat above the edge of Learned Pond. The pond was very deep in spots and had a sandy beach at the far side. We weren't supposed to go down to the pond during lunch or recess, but with no fence to stop us, we did. One warm September, at lunchtime, a boy from the special education class somehow got himself out on a raft, far from shore. We heard him calling for help, so we all ran down the hillside to the edge of the pond.

"Who is that?"

"How did he get out there?"

"Why doesn't swim back?"

An older boy said, "His name is Dino and I bet he can't swim."

We churned up and down the shoreline searching for a better view when one boy picked up a stone and threw it. He missed, but soon more boys started throwing stones. My friend, Bobby Cox, shouted at the boys to stop and pushed some of them, but they kept at it.

Dino drifted out far enough that the stones fell short, until one stone hit him with a thud right over the heart. Dino sank to his knees, and we all fell silent. Then a boy from the ninth grade, Skipper Trudeau, took off his shoes, dove in, and swam out. It took Skipper a long time to reach Dino and the raft. He had trouble keeping Dino calm as the raft kept tipping from side to side. Skipper was strong, but he had to struggle hard to push a frantic Dino and the raft slowly to shore. By the time they stumbled out of the water, a teacher, Mr. Fiendell, was waiting. Mr. Fiendell shouted at all of us to get back up the bank and into school. He corralled Dino, who was on his knees, shaking and sobbing. Skipper stood off aways, dazed, by himself. He didn't look like someone who had just saved a boy.

We marshaled ourselves back up onto the playground where all of us milled around and repeated to each other our eyewitness accounts. Details piled upon details. Dino's calls became screams. A few stone throwers became dozens. One detail remained the same: Only one stone hit Dino; it hit him on the heart; and it was Skipper who threw it. I didn't believe it because how could someone who did something so brave, as what Skipper did, do something so bad?

My mother said that good people often do bad things that they regret, and then try to make up for them, but she couldn't explain why they did them in the first place.

. . . .

Our farm, like most, was a place for roughhouse teasing. As the only child on the farm, I was good focus for the men to have their fun. The Boss made it plain to them and all around that she had her eyes peeled and if they ever got out of hand, they would wish they hadn't. Of course, the men rendered that into a taunt about how I couldn't take care of myself.

One day Bob, working in the dairy, asked me to help him clean one of the big glass-lined vats we used to pasteurize the milk. I slid on rubber boots and gloves, took a brush, and climbed in. As soon as I did, Bob slammed the metal cover down on me and stuck a hose in the opening where the pipes fit. I screamed in terror at the gushing sound, being drenched with water, trapped inside, bent in half in the pitch-black vat.

He held me in the vat for only a few seconds, and when he lifted the lid, he grinned and said, "I suppose you'll go crying to your grandmother now."

I didn't. I didn't know how I could get even, but I wasn't going to be a little kid who tattled. Later that summer, during haying time, I was working in the hayloft using a short pole with a V-shaped metal wedge on the end to hook the fresh bales as they tumbled off the conveyor, and then hauled them to the side for stacking. The hayloft provided a home to a squadron of brown bats. The thud of the tumbling bales always disturbed them into wild, zigzagging flights around the hayloft. I wasn't afraid of them, but just out of protective reflex, I would swing my pole when one came flashing close. One day, as I was finishing a load, I hit one and it landed at my feet. I picked it up and folded its wings back so I could hold it in one hand. It was alive and ferociously biting at the air with its fangs. I climbed down the ladder from the loft and went to the dairy looking for Bob—I knew he was afraid of bats. I found him sweeping out the narrow boiler room, and I saw right away that I had him trapped.

"Hey Bob!" I called, and pointed the writhing bat straight at him.

He dropped the broom and pushed his hands out, palms toward me. He yelled, "No, no no," over and over and cringed back into the space alongside the black boiler tank. He wrapped his arms around himself and turned away from me, screaming.

I realized I had done a bad thing. I waved and shouted to him over his screams that I was leaving and ran into the farmyard to let the bat go.

I was sorry for what I did and sorry that Bob never teased me again.

. . . .

My part beagle, part pointer, Scratch, wasn't mean enough to be a watchdog and hardly seemed bright enough to be much of a hunter. If we came across a rabbit while we were walking to the river, he was as likely to backtrack it into the brush as he was to chase it. He wasn't afraid of strangers or other dogs or the cows, but he was possessed by one fear that took me a while to recognize—he was afraid of the dark. If we were fishing and the shadows began to spread out across the water, he would give out moans and whimpers and walk impatiently in circles like a dog pleading to go outside. The first time he walked off and left me I thought he was just tired, but I caught on to the pattern.

When he took off, Scratch would slink away with his tail down, in a crouch as fast as he could, though he wouldn't actually run, heading for the farmyard where we always kept the lights on. He looked sort of funny moving like that, and I suspected he was hangdog about his fear. I would find him there, contented, as though nothing was wrong. I asked Dr. Slade, the vet we had for our cows, if he had ever heard of a dog being afraid of the dark. He said that dogs, like people, could be afraid of lots of things, though he had never heard of a case such as this.

. . . .

I almost never went shopping downtown with my mother, but one day she said she wanted to show me something. We parked near Garino's Appliances where five or six people stood looking in the window. When we got closer, I saw that they were watching a television. I don't remember what was on, but I was pleased to join the crowd. We were all standing around a big white, plaster dog that Garino's kept out for advertising. A few rich kids in my class used to tell each other, using loud voices, what they watched on television the night before. My mother went inside the store and stayed for a long time. When she came out, I asked her what she did in there.

"We saved up a lot during the war and I we're making money now."+ she said. "No reason the Boss and I should be chipping ice or wringing out and hanging clothes when we can get refrigerators and washing machines to do it. And while I was at it, I decided we should have a television." I snapped my head up.

She beamed down at me and mussed my hair. When I asked what all that cost, she said we didn't have to pay for it today; we could pay ten dollars a month and bring the money in clipped to the coupons she showed me. I thought on the ride home that somehow it didn't seem right, but I was happy we were getting a television.

The Boss made her "hard face" when my mother told her about what we bought, so I knew how she felt about all this buying. She felt that ever since the war ended, people were spending money they didn't have. One radio commercial always set her off. Kay Jewelers offered to sell jewelry on credit with a singing jingle that played over and over on the radio.

It's OK to owe Kay till payday.
Your promise to pay is OK with Kay.
For gifts and watches and diamond rings,
Come in and see all the beautiful things.
Oh! It's OK to owe Kay till payday,
Your promise to pay is OK with Kay.
OK, OK, OK!

"Can you imagine! Going into debt to buy jewelry," she would exclaim.

Garino's delivered everything the next day. The washer fit down in the cellar, but Pop, Charlie, and I had to nestle the refrigerator into a corner of the vestibule. Garino's man helped us set up the television in the sitting room at the end of the hall on the second floor. Garino's man called it a "TV." We stood gawking while he twisted the antenna all around until we could see a picture. He explained that it was a test pattern and it ran during the day before the programs started coming on at 4:00.

That afternoon at 4:00, everyone stopped working and came up to the sitting room, even Evold, the route man from Svea bakery, who was delivering some *toska* tarts for Pop. I could tell it was a special time because the Boss let everyone keep their boots on. The first show was a puppet show for kids and, after a few minutes, everyone mumbled expressions of mild wonder and left to get back to chores.

We evolved our watching habits cooperatively. We all liked the news. For the first time, I began to feel connected to other parts of the country; I could see what it really looked like in Texas or California and hear about what was going on. I liked watching people from other places speak. Not only did they sound different with their accents, but they used different expressions—"We hope how soon it stops, I told y'all that, you can't holler down the rain"—and they had different ways of moving. I tried to mimic them. I watched the news people show films and talk about things from all over the world. A lot of the news stories took place in cities. I had never been to a city except to visit my Aunt Helen in Boston, and she usually sent me home after two days because I tired her out. Some stories told the news of places like Berlin or Tokyo or London. A lot of the news showed President Truman, General Eisenhower, Governor Dever, and others. I began to understand that some people were extremely important because of what they did, though more often than I wanted, I wasn't sure of what that was. What shook me most was that so much could be happening all around me in the world that I didn't know about and so much that I had to find out about.

The Boss liked music shows and *Ed Sullivan*, but really enjoyed being able to see her radio favorite, Arthur Godfrey. We were all anxious to see shows from radio such as *Jack Benny, Henry Aldrich*, and *Truth or Consequences* because we could now see whether the characters really looked like what we imagined. Sometimes we were disappointed. We watched *I Remember Mama*, but Pop often noted that the Hansens were Norwegian. He liked *The Lone Ranger*, mainly because he admired the horsemanship of the rider in the opening sequence.

We didn't watch sports; baseball was on in the afternoon, and we didn't like boxing. The big surprise was how Pop took to watching wrestling. It came on at 10:00 p.m., and even though he had to get up early, he would wait to see if his favorite—a grotesque wrestler called the Swedish Angel—was in a match. No matter how we tried to convince him, Pop would not accept that the whole thing was just a show.

The refrigerator turned out to be a great addition, too. The Boss liked to make up a big bowl of cucumbers in vinegar and salt that she stowed in the refrigerator for us to grab. It had a small, ice-making freezer compartment. My mother made Kool-Aid and poured it into the divided metal trays to make flavored ice cubes. My favorite was grape.

. . . .

One day, when I was opening the big barn door that faced the farmyard, I somehow got a rake jammed. Try as I might, I couldn't pull the rake out, and I couldn't push the door in either direction to free it. Charlie and Pop were standing in the yard, watching. Charlie walked over, gave one big shove to the door, and the rake clattered to the floor inside, freeing the door.

Later that day, Pop asked me to come into the kitchen and give him a hand with something. He and the Boss laid out paper and pencil. He told me he wanted to buy fence for the poison ivy field—as we called it—and needed to know how much we needed. He didn't have the time to figure out how much fence it would take, and I was the only one he could ask. Even though the field was an irregular shape, it wasn't a complicated job: do some even pacing, some measuring allowing for rocks and stumps, and add up the figures. I listened to them describe my task with my head down and put on a serious look. I knew what they were doing, and I didn't want to let on that I knew. Pop figured that I might have been embarrassed by Charlie easily freeing the barn door that I couldn't even budge. So, here was a job Charlie couldn't do and I could.

I don't remember if we ever did fence that poison ivy field.

....

A few days later Charlie called me aside to the barn. "You got to learn how to defend yourself," he said. When I asked why he said, "So's other kids won't push you around." I said how no one pushed me around, but he already had two wads of folded up newspapers he was pushing under my arms.

"Pull your elbows in and hold those close to your sides so's they won't fall out and then put your fists up like this." He got in the same stance, facing me, but without any newspapers, and started circling around me like a boxer. I kept circling to face him. Quick as a flash he flicked a fist out to my cheek and drew it back. Then he did it again, all so fast. "OK, now I want you to take a jab at me with your left hand and get that hand back so fast that you don't drop the newspaper."

I thought I might hit Charlie so I went easy and too slow. The newspaper rattled to the wood floor. "Pick it up and try again. Don't worry about hitting me - that won't happen," he smiled. I tried four or five times before I could jab out a punch and catch the newspaper before it fell. Then he put on canvas work gloves and told me to start really hitting his hands, one then the other. I got so I could snap him pretty hard with my left hand and still keep the newspaper caught, but I dropped the newspaper from under my right arm half the time.

"You hit hard with that right hand, but that's not good enough; you got to be fast." With that he threw a fast left hand over my slow right hand and tagged me a good one right flat on the side of my jaw. I staggered back and he pretended to be wailing away on me.

"You should jab that left to back me out." I did.

Charlie gave me a few more lessons and said I shouldn't run away from a fight, but I'd be better off not to start any.

"You're fast and strong enough, but you don't have it in you to hurt people, and they'll see that."

. . . .

I had great respect for our draft horses, Tom and Jerry. They did what work was asked and seemed to prefer their own company. Gypsy, on the other hand, stomped and whinnied for attention all the time. I never cared to ride horses much, but Laura had one she rode all over the back hills.

My grandmother said of Laura Rawlings, "She'll never be hung for her beauty," but I thought she was pretty enough. Her oval face was simple, with wide-set, blue eyes that sparkled like chips of broken glass. Her hair was simple, too—a short, thick thatch of coppery brown that sat like closed parentheses around her face. She lived on a middling to mean farm in the hills beyond us, and worked hard because her mother wasn't well. She was strong for a girl and owned just a touch of fierceness I could see once in a while. Her voice was clear, and she used small hand motions, waving them when she talked, which was not all that often. Mostly she listened, wearing a slight frown. When she did smile, her whole face changed, and I guessed she hadn't much practice at it. Back in the first grade, other kids teased her about being poor and from the hills. Some kids said she was part witch like everyone up in the hills, but when the war got going, that stopped because we all felt we were on the same side. She was the fastest runner in our grade.

She knew I liked to fish, so she told me I should ride over and go with her up the fire road to the dam. She always rode bareback, and I wanted to look like a good rider, so I set to go bareback to impress her. Our Gypsy was a big, quirky, chestnut mare. She hated anything near her ears, so you had to go slow rigging her up. She was neck reined, so you didn't hold the reins one in each hand, you held them tied together and leaned them into her neck in the direction you wanted her to go. And she was afraid of bridges.

The June day opened gray-green and soft. All went well on the ride over, even crossing the drainage bridge at the far end of our place. I showed up feeling like a real cowboy. Laura, wearing a white shirt, looked me over and nodded to the fire road. We rode side by side, small chatting about our farms. After a while, she stopped and pointed across me to the left at some flowers.

"Lady slippers. It's against the law to pick them."

"I know," I said. "I was sitting behind you when Miss Marshall told us."

When we started moving again, Laura kept her left hand like she was still pointing but sort of palm up, like she was waiting for something. I didn't catch on until she shook her hand a little and frowned. I reached over and took it, and so we rode.

One thing I already knew about myself was that I hated not knowing things. Everybody said I was smart, but I knew I was really dumb because I didn't know how things worked or why things happened or what made people do things. This time, I was happy to learn.

As we rode up the last rise to the dam, a few but steady drops of rain pattered the leaves and touched our hands. She stopped and gave me a look I couldn't figure then and can't now. She dropped my hand.

"I put clothes on the line. Momma can't get them in, so I gotta go."

We turned our horses, and on impulse, I leaned over and planted a truly clumsy peck on her cheek. I know I saw a blush in the second before she rode off. I wondered what she thought about the fact that neither one of us had brought a fishing rod.

I was moving Gypsy at a good clip in the steady rain on the way home, but this time when we got to the drainage bridge, she stopped short, dead still. With nothing to grab onto, I went over her shoulder onto my back into the muddy ditch. I wasn't hurt. I got up and led her over the bridge. When I reached up to put the reins over her head so I could remount, she cried a high whinny and shook me off as soon as I got next to her ears. I caught up to her and tried again, but when I raised the reins near her ears she bolted another few yards away. We went on like that, in the rain, our six feet ka-sloshing in the wet hay stubble, all the way across the lower hay field. I gave up and, drenched, led her rest of the way up to the farmyard.

I found Pop standing out of the rain in the barn doorway. I figured out he had been watching me and my long trials with Gypsy's ears. He squinted his bright blue eyes to make me stop, came out from the doorway, and not saying a word, took the reins from me. He untied them real quick and reached around Gypsy's neck, far from her ears, and just as quick retied them. We stood still there for a minute in the rain. He maybe was thinking he had the dumbest grandson in the world who couldn't have figured that out, but all he said was, "Dry her off, *sot pojke*. And go change. We've got chores." He turned back into the barn, most likely hiding a big smile.

. . . .

In the fifth grade, I owned a bicycle that I could ride to school so long as I stayed on the back road along the river. I made a plan. I rigged up a fishing pole from a busted-off radio antenna from one of our trucks and stashed it in a thick clump of pines beside the river. My plan was to stop on my way to school, scratch up a few worms from under the pine needles, and fish for a few minutes. The first day I tried, I stayed so long it was too late to go to school, so I spent all day fishing and catching crayfish. When I got home, I slid right into chores and everything went OK. A few days later, I did the same thing and missed another day, but this time, when I was putting my bike away, the Boss stepped out through the screen door and told me she got a call from Mr. Jones, the truant officer, about where was I. I shuffled up to her.

"What did you say?" I asked.

"I told him what I knew was that Pop was mowing a piece over on the other side of Route 9 today."

"Did you say I was with him?"

"No," she said, "That would have been lying."

I didn't have to say I wouldn't do it again, and I didn't have to say I was sorry. I did find out that you can lie with silence.

. . . .

The business was grow-ing. We milked forty cows and fed fifteen heifers in Brewer's old barn now that he only kept orchards. We called our best milker Big Red. Pop weighed her milk all the time and had one of our drivers drop off jars of her milk at the state of-fice in Natick to check the amount of butter fat. Twice a year, he sent his records to the American Guern-sey Association, and they would send back a certificate with a wax seal on it. One time a man with a camera came and took Big Red's picture to put in their magazine. My grandmother had him take lots of pictures of Pop and me with Big Red.

Pop was very proud of having registered Guernseys. He loved to tell me that the milk was golden colored because it was so rich and that it tasted better than milk from other kinds of cows. He showed me through the glass bottles that the cream line came down further than other milk. The test results from the state office got printed in the newspaper and they showed that Pop was right. The American Guernsey Association gave us the OK to call our milk "golden Guernsey." He always posted the test results in the milk room. Uncle Carl asked Pop if he posted them in there because he thought the cows could read them.

We now rented Brewer's hay fields, but even those weren't enough, so we added a new feed. Once a week, Uncle Carl and I would drive our big hay truck to Continental Bakeries in the old factory section of Watertown to pick up day-old bread. The men at the bakery always gave us a crate of donuts and pastries as an extra, and on the way home we stuffed ourselves. I had fun unloading the truck because I threw the huge boxes of bread around like I was a strong man. The bread worked pretty well, but it took up a lot of room, and we couldn't count on it because once in a while Continental would tell us not to come in.

As the only kid on the farm, I was a good source of amusement for the men. They especially liked it when, after haying in the big field to the west, I would race the truck back to the barn. They would stand out in the yard and cheer me on. I'm pretty sure that the few times I won it was because Uncle Carl would slowly ease off the gas a little as we got up into the yard.

While I wasn't old enough to drive on the road for chores like picking up the bread, I did drive on the farm. When I got strong enough to buck bales onto our flatbed, I taught myself a trick. The old blue Chevy had a pull-out throttle choke that I set to a slow walking speed, and then I put the truck on a path between two rows of bales. The bales were two feet wide, two feet tall, and four feet long. Most of them weighed 40 to 50 pounds. I was able to walk alongside the truck, buck a few bales up on my knee, to my forearm, and to the truck in one move. When I had a few up on the truck I'd jump up on the truck and stack them, hop down, and do it again until I had to turn the truck around. I could bring up two or three loads in an afternoon.

Sitting around supper one evening after I had been haying, Uncle Carl told the family, "I saw the damnedest thing today." They all asked what it was and he said, "I thought I saw someone loading and stacking bales all alone. Stacked the whole truckload."

"Couldn't be," said Charlie. "Nobody's that strong."

"Your eyes are bad," Pop said sipping his soup.

"I know what I saw," Uncle Carl confirmed.

The Boss looked up. "Who was it?"

"I can't be sure, but it could have been Laura Rawlings—she's a strong girl, you know."

....

Kids at school called the summer "vacation." I thought of it as my real life. *Real life* was farming and striking on the routes and fishing and there wasn't anything better than that. I so dreaded that first cool August evening warning of summer's end that, for one summer, I made up a schedule for every day so that I wouldn't waste any time. I even had it broken down for every half hour. My mother said she had never heard of anybody doing that but she said she understood. At first I felt good about my schedule; I had proof that I wasn't wasting any time. But after a while, I realized that summer was going to end no matter what I tried to do to hold on to it.

Summer brought me joy. Every day, I felt pure and simple delight. Walking the dirt tractor paths to the river on a still afternoon and feeling the dust puff through my toes made me smile. Every day seemed like it could stretch out into a whole summer of blue afternoons. I loved the smells of summer: fresh-cut hay, a cornfield, the peppery, wild grasses that grew along our stone walls.

Everything I did stirred me. I fished in an early morning mist or a shimmering summer evening. I picked huckleberries on the scrubby-pasture hillside. I spent hours daydreaming in the monotony of a droning tractor raking hay. I caught crayfish in the small brook under cool, drenching shade. I hayed, got sweaty and covered with hay chaff, and then rinsed it all off with a running dive into the river. At the end of the day, I captured fireflies in a milk bottle and set it beside my bed.

Now that I had a bike, I went all over looking for new places to fish. One of our milk routes traveled alongside a high, perfectly straight stone wall, not like the ragged ones on the farm. My father told me that behind that wall was a place called "Raceland," owned by a very rich man named John Macomber.

Raceland   Courtesy of Framinham History Center

He lived in a great stone house and had his own kennel with lots of dogs. My father said the place was so big that people came and raced horses around a dirt track. I heard that Mr. Macomber was able to get the MDC people, who ran the reservoir system, to break off a good-sized braid of the river to feed though the middle of his Raceland, and I figured it had to be full of fish.

One day on the milk route, I saw a dark plank gate in the stone wall standing open. That afternoon, I rode my bike through that gate into Raceland. I can't say to this day I ever felt anything like I felt my first time inside those stone walls.

I came to a stop on a gray, powdered stone drive as wide as a town road. I looked to my left and saw an oval racetrack. The track itself was light-brown dirt and laid out around a thick grass infield. Sections of head-high hedges broke my clear view.

Straight ahead, I looked up at a three-story red brick building with bright-white shutters and trim, capped with a cupola. The weather vane atop the cupola showed an angel with flowing hair blowing a long horn. I pedaled up, and facing me at the driveway level were seven garage doors, but I suspicioned they might be fancy stable shields. The flat apron of powdered stone in front of the doors showed no tire tracks or hoof prints.

The drive divided around the brick building. I chose to go left, toward the racetrack, and found that more drives wound all around, in and out, under giant weeping willows. I saw the edge of a golf course laid out toward a far wall. The thickest, greenest grass I ever saw ran carpet smooth right down to the edge of the water. It was quiet as a cemetery. I felt sure that in that quiet, just the sound of my bike on the stone would bring someone out to put a stop to me. Far off, I could see a steep slate roof, but I didn't see or hear anyone.

I hardly had any excuse if I got caught, but I counted on whoever caught me having a soft spot for boys fishing, even where they shouldn't. I laid my bike down, made my way to the edge of the water, and scouted out a nice pool, the kind fish like. The best place for me to stand looked to be near some cat-o-nine tails a little upstream. I no sooner made my move when three screaming swans – necks stretched out, giant wings spread - came flying at me out from behind the cat-o-nine tails. One bit me good in the neck, and the others pecked and slapped at me hard with their wings. I dropped my rod and ran for my bike, but they stayed on me screeching, pecking, and swatting. Dogs began to bark. I was keeping my eyes closed in the thick of my battle when the swans suddenly changed from screeching like banshees to squawking like geese and left off of me. I peeked open my eyes; I saw two brown dogs with shiny fur making on a dead run for the swans who were now half flying to the water.

When they landed out in the water, the dogs pranced up and down the grassed shore, stalking the swans and wagging their tails like mad.

"It's their big game," a voice behind me said. A thin, gray-haired man, older than Pop, sat in the driver's seat of a blue convertible car with four doors. He had on a gray suit and wore a black tie. "How did you get in here, and what are you doing besides upsetting my swans and my dogs?" he asked. He spoke in a stern way but not mad.

"The gate on Salem End Road was open. I was going to go fishing."

"What's your name?"

"Douglas Peterson." I could see that didn't satisfy him, so I jerked my thumb over my shoulder toward home and said, "Hillcrest Farm."

"Are you Enoch Peterson's son?"

"Grandson," I said.

For some time, he shifted his gaze here and there, finally settling it on me. "You can fish here, but don't bring anyone with you. Clear?" His eyes behind his glasses shone blue-gray and bright. I nodded yes. "There's a wire swing gate on Badger Road – use that. You can walk it from your farm." Then he drove off. I thanked him, but I don't think he heard me.

When I got back home, I stood in the kitchen and showed everyone the marks of my fight at Raceland, and told them about Mr. Macomber letting me fish there. They all said he was the richest man in town.

"One of Mr. Macomber's horses is like to be worth more than our whole herd of Guernseys," Pop said.

Other times when I fished at Raceland, Mr. Macomber would come out in his big convertible and slow down to watch me. I would wave, but he never did. He would slow down and look right at me and I would tense up, worried that he would stop and tell me to leave, but he just glided by. Sometimes, though, I felt he was waiting for me.

I could also bike to a shallow pond that sat in a wooded field near town. Some of the kids used it for skating in the winter, and I could always catch one or two catfish or blue gill if I fished there. In the spring, near the end of the sixth grade, when I thought winter had tipped over and it was warm enough for the ice to be off, I made my first fishing trip of the year to the pond. I pulled up on my bike and saw the fishing pond was gone. So were the woods. The whole field was torn up. Construction shacks with the name Campanelli on them clustered at one end while some old Army bulldozers and steam shovels moved in short, halting routes around mounds of tan soil. I could make out where several foundations were being dug and where the roads would be laid. I rode around trying to locate the pond site. I couldn't imagine making a whole fishing pond disappear.

When I got back to the farm, I found my father in the kitchen counting out his day's receipts and told him what I had found, that I had lost a place to fish.

"They probably capped the spring that fed the pond and piped the water into the Sudbury River. Land that close to town is all going to go over to Campanelli houses," he told me.

. . . .

I came out from milking one afternoon and found my father, Uncle Carl, and some of the drivers standing around a new truck. It was called a Divco, and you drove it standing up. It looked like a miniature bus made especially for delivering milk. With business good, we needed two more trucks, and one of the old Internationals was pretty shot, so my father made a deal with the man who sold the Divcos to let us buy all three. He took the old International in for trade and let us pay on time for the rest we owed.

My family and the other farmers around us had bad things to say about the farmers in Vermont. They said Vermont farmers didn't take care about when their cows had calves, so sometimes their cows all started giving fresh milk at the same time, and that brought down the price. Now, after the war shortages, farms up there had new tractors and better refrigeration and were producing even more milk. Vermont farmers didn't have many customers near them, so they had to sell their milk to people from the big companies, like Sealtest and National Dairy, who would sell it in the cities. One night, after supper, Uncle Carl read us a story from the newspaper that told how the farmers up there thought they weren't being paid enough for their milk, and so they had started the Vermont Dairymen's League. Now, for the second spring in a row, it said, they put out so much milk that the prices fell way down. The farmers in the League were so furious that they poured their milk down the drain rather than sell it to the big dairies. We couldn't afford to do that, and we would lose all our customers forever if we did, so we had to live with the low prices and the worry about what would happen next spring.

"It's crazy," Pop said. "Now, the more milk you make, the less money you make."

. . . .

A tall, black-haired lady named Grace Krill drove into the farm one hazy afternoon to talk with the Boss and Pop. Her family built houses. She knew all about who owned what land and who bought how many acres and what it sold for. The Boss saw the car and came out to wait on the top step. As I did when anyone came to visit, I found a place to stand where I could hear what the talk was about. Grace parked her gray Buick and got out to stand in front of the Boss.

"With the boys coming back and starting families, everybody is looking for a place to build a house," she said. "Just about all the farms in Sherborn are going – Miriam, Dexter, Brown. Dairy farming is tough these days. Dave Sundstrom got rid of his place over the winter. A whole new development is going in. We paid him a fair price considering much of his place was wet. I wanted you to know that."

The Boss told Grace Krill that she knew for a fact that Dave Sundstrom wasn't happy with how things turned out.

"Grace, we're not intending to sell," I heard the Boss say.

Grace Krill straightened, sending a signal the talk was over.

"Myrtle, I just stopped by to let you and Enoch know that these days we're always looking for land." No one shook hands or anything; Grace got in her car and drove off.

. . . .

I looked forward to visiting my cousins in town. I especially liked it when we scrounged around the neighborhood and made fairly workable guns out of blocks of wood, clothespins, and strips of inner tube. One day, while we were wandering around the streets and alleys playing war and searching for anything we could break, a wild-eyed man jumped out at us, screaming and waving his arms. I recognized him: He was a distant cousin, Guisto. He jumped toward my cousin Dick, then toward me. My cousin John, the calmest of us, stepped in between.

"Guisto!" John barked. Patting himself on the chest and pointing to the rest of us he said, "*Cugini*, cousins."

Guisto calmed down, lolling his arms around his sides, twisting, moaning. John approached him a ways and called out to us over his shoulder, "He just wants to go home." I knew the story; Guisto was wounded early in the war and spent years in Army hospitals. While he was away, his family moved two streets over. When he came home from the hospital, he could not accept that his old house was no longer his home.

He would stand in front of his old house and cry for hours on end, demanding that the new owners give back his house. All our family efforts to get him to stop, to convince him of the new situation, did not work. Kids got hustled away when he came out because he could be frightening. Then one day Guisto was gone. No one would say where he went. The sight of his tortured face and the sound of his anguished cries remain vivid to me.

. . . .

Making his own commotion, my father rushed into the big kitchen all excited and spread a newspaper out on the table.

"Look! General Motors is building a factory here in Framingham. Out towards Holliston. They'll make Buicks, Oldsmobiles, and Pontiacs. This means a lot of people and money coming to town."

For the next year, the newspaper was full of what the factory would mean, about how many people would work there and how, now, lots of other businesses would come to Framingham. The paper said that nothing this big had ever happened anywhere around here. People guessed we would need more houses and roads and that Framingham would need to build more schools.

Some new kids did come to school. One of them was Holly Sheehan, the factory manager's daughter. She was the first person I ever met who was from California. She made friends with a few girls right away, but some of the others thought she was stuck-up. They gossiped about her bright-colored clothes and short hair and how she lived in Singletary Lane, near Mr. Macomber's Raceland.

One day, I was wandering across the far edge of the playground where it turned into woods when Holly Sheehan, wearing a red scarf, came walking in quick steps straight toward me.

She smiled hello and then said, "Would you like to come to a party at my house on Saturday?" When I said yes, she smiled a sunny smile, said it started at seven o'clock, and walked back toward the school. On the school bus that afternoon, I told Laura how surprised I was about being invited to Holly's party seeing how I didn't really know her or anything.

When she got up to get off the bus, Laura turned to me and said, "She asked me about you. I told her you are sincere."

The night of the party, I put on khakis and a tan sweater the Boss had knit for me. "Where you going all dolled up?" Uncle Carl asked.

"I'm going to a party in Singletary Lane."

"You wearing that calf-turd, yellow sweater to a party?" he laughed.

"It's not calf-turd yellow. It's tan," the Boss called. "You look fine," she said to me.

My mother swarmed around me fixing my collar and brushing my hair. They stood side by side at the door as I got into the pickup with my father. My mother and the Boss had fussed over me, I guess, because it was the first party I was going to since I had gone to little kid birthday parties.

When we got to Singletary Lane and could see the high stone wall around Raceland, my father asked, "You still sneaking in there to fish?" He knew well enough that Mr. Macomber was still letting me fish there. "Richest man in Framingham," which is what he always said about Mr. Macomber.

Holly's driveway, a car-wide notch in a row of tall privet hedges, led to a brick house with brass lights that looked like old lanterns on each side of the door. Holly answered as soon as I knocked and took my hand and led me toward the sound of voices rising from a big cram of people—adults, older kids, and kids my age – standing around talking and laughing in a room as big as the school assembly hall.

She told me that she had to help her mother and that I should walk around and say hello. I stood next to a group of older boys who were telling each other quick snatches of things amid lots of laughing. I noticed that the collars on their shirts had buttons, I guessed to keep them from popping up.

One group of four boys about my age took long note of me before one of them asked who I was. I told him who I was and that I went school with Holly. "Do you ski?" The tallest one, named Terry, asked. Before I could say no, another boy asked if I played hockey and another boy slid in a question about whether I caddied at the country club.

"I work on my family's farm, Hillcrest Farm out on Route 9," I explained.

They considered that for a minute, then one of them asked, "Do you go to the Red Sox games?" I said no, but that I once went to a Braves game on the Civic League bus.

Terry said, "Oh, the Braves. I guess you know they're leaving Boston?"

I didn't know but pretended that I did. Then they closed up their circle and went back to talking and laughing about things at St. Sebastian's, their school. They had smiles in their eyes. After that, I wandered around with a Coke in my hand, never stopping, listening in on people talking about tennis or sailing or trips they had taken or other matters we never talked about at home. Some people would look my way and give me a quick smile I took to be an invitation to say something, but I didn't know what to say that wouldn't make me seem dumb.

At nine thirty, I found Holly in the kitchen with her mother. The kitchen was a big, square room with copper hinges on the cabinet doors and copper pots hanging from overhead rails. Holly introduced us. Mrs. Sheehan stopped her work, brushed her hands on her yellow apron, and hurried toward me.

"Oh, the Douglas Peterson I've heard so much about!" she said, throwing a smile toward Holly. Mrs. Sheehan looked like a movie star with long red hair, pale skin. and a bright, white smile of perfect teeth. I stammered a "good night" and "thanks" that got smothered in words about how she was sorry we didn't have a chance to spend time together.

Holly took my arm in both her hands, walked me to the door, and thanked me for coming. "We'll get to talk more next time," she promised.

On the way home in the truck with my father, I wondered if any of those boys I talked with had ever been sad about anything. When he asked me how was the party, I told my father everyone was nice to me.

On Monday, before school, Holly found me and took my hands. "Everybody at the party said they liked you. Did you have a good time?"

When I said yes, she smiled a big smile, squeezed my hands, and said, "I really liked your sweater."

That night, before supper, when I told my mother and the Boss what happened, my mother said I should invite Holly out to the farm.

"Girls like horses, you know."

When we went back to school after Christmas, Holly wasn't in class. Laura told me Holly went off to private school in Wellesley.

. . . .

The Boss heard the news that Jim Cowells had gotten himself arrested. Jim went to school with my father and got known around as a kid dunked in small troubles. He failed to finish school, drove cars too fast, and never had any money. That changed when he joined the fire department. We judged that the excitement suited him and that the older firemen settled him down. He came to put out a grass fire at the farm once.

He joined the Army and became a paratrooper as soon as the war started. His name made the papers when he was wounded in Italy from shots fired by our own side. He came home leaning on a cane he would need for the rest of his life.

He also came home to find that his wife, Carol, had taken a job at Dennison Paper. She had started on the finishing line, packaging boxes of white labels with red edges, but soon became the boss of the line on the night shift. Word was that the pay as a supervisor plus night-shift bonus totaled as much as Jim had made as a fireman. She enjoyed the money and the independence and felt she could make a good career for herself. Jim made it known that he saw a different future. He expected her to stay home and have children the way women always did. Carol told him that things had changed while he was away. She and lots of other women she knew had gone to work and learned that they could handle life on their own. The OPA had frozen wages and so Dennison Paper, in order to attract workers, had started offering Blue Cross medical insurance and nursery care for workers' children.

The Boss said that "Women found out that they like their new roles. Their husbands are just going to have to adapt."

For Jim, it was a double hit; the war set him back while it shoved Carol forward. He took up drinking and drifted from job to job, none amounting to much due to his long weekends and short temper. He came by to ask my father if we had any work for him, but we had no farm job for a man, even a friend, on a cane.

They arrested Jim outside his own house. The police found him staggering around on his front lawn, waving a gun. It turned out that he had brought the gun home as a souvenir from Italy, and it didn't even work.

"Jim Cowells came home up against tall walls with a short ladder," the Boss said. "We're not going back to the wat thing were."

PART THREE

MID-CENTURY

The course of the country shifted. Cities were emptying their residents out into the suburbs on brand new highways. As if to replenish the losses of war, our birthrates vaulted an additional million a year.

Desperate to put WW II behind us, we tried to shut out Korea as a disruption. Our waning admiration for General McArthur transformed into our growing disdain for Senator McCarthy.

The early '50s were not the Happy Days of television. We were forced to accept a new equilibrium with Communism and nuclear potential, constructing a constant grayness. Predictably, most Americans adapted and moved ahead. Inevitably, some were left behind.

After Christmas, my mother sat me down in my room and told me she had taken a part-time factory job with Bay State Abrasives. She had been at loose ends for some time, and I knew she felt farm work and house chores were boring.

"There isn't enough housework to do now, and I'm no farmer. Your Aunt Esther and Aunt Theresa and lots of their friends have all gone to work. There are lots of jobs for women now, and they can earn good money and get insurance." When I didn't say anything, she patted me on the shoulder and left.

I could tell the rest of the family was uneasy about her working in a factory, but the Boss said how we could make good use of the extra money and I could be covered under her health insurance.

. . . .

During 1950, some people in Framingham decided it was a good idea to celebrate the town being 250 years old. Raymond Callahan, my friend's father and the publisher of the *Framingham News*, took on the job to run the celebration. At school, we did one project after another about what is was like back in 1700 and about everything that had happened over the years. Stores put old pictures in their windows, and when they gave back change, they passed out small pieces of cardboard printed to look like money, called "wooden nickels," which you could change for five cents at any bank in town. The newspaper ran stories about historical things every day. The town sold a history book to help raise money for all the concerts and fairs to be held. The celebration ended with a big parade where some people came from Framlingham, England and sat on the reviewing stand. Framlingham is where our town name came from, people said. During the parade, I carried one corner of a huge American flag. A man standing at the curb tossed in a quarter as we passed. When the parade was over, I asked the man who collected the flag from us what I should do with the quarter. "Keep it," he said, but that didn't seem right. I didn't know who to give it to, so I put it in my draw with my Red Sox baseball.

The most important thing for me about the anniversary happened at Mr. Macomber's Raceland. One day in June, I rode in and found four big white trucks parked in front of the stables. I saw a dozen or so men all dressed alike in green work clothes busying themselves around the race-track and calling out to each other some things I couldn't hear. I didn't feel brave enough to go ask what was going on because I always felt my fishing permission was very slender and subject to being taken from me. I went fishing, and sure enough, a skinny man in green came walking down to me, motioning me to get out and come to him.

"Who said you could fish here?" he asked.

"Mr. Macomber said I could," I answered.

"Well, Mr. Macomber has closed the place for the next week. He said no one is allowed in. Get on your bike, now."

The man wasn't mad, but he frowned and looked stern and serious.

When I got back to the farm, the Boss was sitting in the far end of the living room, among her African violets, reading, a box of chocolates on the table at her side. I told her what happened.

"They probably ran you off because those men were getting Raceland ready for the Boston Pops to come and play the big anniversary concert." When I asked if we could go, she said, "It's by invitation only, and your good friend, Mr. John R. Macomber, hasn't invited us."

The Korean War started right in the middle of Framingham's 250th anniversary in June of 1950. In the beginning, I thought the war wasn't going to amount to much. The whole of the United Nations was going to fight against a small country named North Korea. But the war grew greater, like a big stain slowly spreads out from a small leak. Soon, some men got called back into the service. The most famous for us was Ted Williams of the Red Sox.

My mother and the Boss complained about prices going up, but they were just as afraid that new price controls would be followed by rationing.

"I thought we were through with all this," my mother said.

The war turned into a stalemate, and President Truman fired General McArthur. I didn't know you could fire a general, but the news said General McArthur planned to disobey President Truman and that could not be allowed.

A year after he was fired, General Douglas McArthur came to Framingham and visited some newly wounded soldiers at Cushing Hospital, our veterans' hospital built during the war. He spoke to a very big crowd gathered in front of Nevins Hall and repeated what he said in all his speeches: "Old soldiers never die, they just fade away." Mr. Victor Galvani, the First Selectman, gave the general a clock from Telechron in Ashland, but did not give him a parade.

It seemed to me most people wanted the war to be over in a hurry. They were enjoying the boom times, getting back to normal, and didn't want anything to get in their way. People didn't talk about Korea the way they talked about the world war. When Korea ended, people wanted to forget all about it, but the idea of Communism—and Communists—had entered everyone's lives. Being patriotic now meant being anti-Communist. Advertisements in the newspapers and magazines warned about Communist spies. One movie I saw was called, *I Was a Communist for the FBI*, and it became a television series.

I worked hard to sort out for myself if what had been right and wrong was changing. I started to hear so many disagreements, not like during the war when everyone seemed to be pulling together. I figured that people had so enjoyed the thrill of feeling safe after the war that Korea was a bad reminder, and they were anxious to push it aside.

My father said it was a lot more than that. He felt my Uncle Faust had put his finger on it when he said that people were so busy enjoying themselves that they didn't want to see what was coming. "We've had five years of sunshine, now the clouds are coming back."

The clouds, for most people, were just shadows. People frowned, with quiet concern, at Senator McCarthy's hearings in Congress. All the new talk about Communists living among us would get people excited for a while, but when nothing seemed to happen, people got used to it. Even when two spies went on trial, people said, "Well, that's just New York."

The atomic bomb and the new, yellow radiation triangles weren't ignored, but only a few people gave any thought to bomb shelters and even fewer built them. People learned to live with shadows and dove into the 1950s.

"Whistling past the graveyard," the Boss called it.

. . . .

Uncle Carl and I were washing down the dairy floor when my father came in and said he had some bad news.

"A&P has dropped us and gone to Sealtest." He looked at the two of us to be sure it sank in. "I've known Jimmy, the store manager, from before the war, but he said there was nothing he could do. All the A&P stores had to go to Sealtest and get the lower price."

Uncle Carl blamed the Vermont farmers and their cheap milk.

"Jimmy also told me we better start homogenizing our milk like Sealtest. Customers don't like shaking the bottle to mix up the cream and still end up with skim milk at the end."

I looked to Uncle Carl. "Is homogenizing hard to do?"

"No, it just costs money for two machines and some piping."

We had the homogenizer put in right away. We printed up a note for the drivers to leave with customers asking them if they wanted their milk regular or homogenized. The drivers made jokes and laughed about how from now on we had to mark down which customers were regular and which ones were homos. It fell to Pop to tell me what the homo joke was all about. It was always pretty plain to me where calves, and so babies, came from, and I knew what Charlie was getting at when he teased me about Laura Rawlings. But I had to ask Pop to keep going over this homo idea, and he could see I was really upset.

I was traipsing behind him cleaning up the barn when I said, "I can't see how I didn't already know about something as big as that."

"You don't know lots of things yet. You'll always be finding out."

. . . .

None of our school playgrounds was big enough for us to play baseball, and no one lived near enough to the farm to get up a game. When I rode my bike to town to see my cousins, we would play at Butterworth Field. My cousin Ronny's father, Lindy, sometimes stopped by and watched us. He told me I should play in the outfield because I was fast and could get to a lot of fly balls. I knew I wasn't very good at second base, and Uncle Lindy was trying to give me a good reason to give it up. One summer, he had a job building a motel not far from the farm and passed by every day. He told my mother he saw me haying and said, "They work that kid like a mule."

Some of the businessmen in Framingham joined together to form the Civic League. They built a building with a basketball court; they put together sports programs; and they were part of the "knothole gang." If you were a member, 50 cents bought you a seat on a bus and a ticket to a Boston Braves game. The Braves weren't as good or as popular as the Red Sox, but in 1948 they went to the World Series while the Red Sox lost out on going by one game.

The Braves needed to give away 50 cent seats to get people to attend, and even that didn't work well. Adding to the Braves's problem, the population of Boston started to fall very fast after the war because, as Grace Krill had told us, people could now afford to buy houses and move out to the newly built suburbs.

With low attendance and people moving out of Boston, Lou Perini, the owner of the Braves, finally had enough. Even though he was from Framingham, he moved the Braves to Milwaukee in 1953.

The Red Sox were not part of the knothole gang.

. . . .

In the spring before I turned sixteen, my father told me to get in his pickup, that he wanted to show me something. We drove in silence over the river to a lowland farm owned by the Blood family and pulled down into a slim crescent of land with turned dirt that looked like chocolate.

"How would you like to make some extra money this summer?"

I said I would because I wanted to buy a car. He opened his door and motioned for me to do the same. We started walking slowly, toeing at the plowed dirt.

"Blood says his Junior took a job at the GM plant. Without Junior, he can't work all his place, so he's offered this piece to us plowed and harrowed for two hundred dollars."

"What would we grow?" I asked.

"Jerry Gardella at Bay State Produce tells me he hasn't been able to get enough tomatoes for the stores he sells to in Boston. I could see us growing a lot of tomatoes off this nice piece of land, but I can't do it by myself."

I told him I could help, but he said help wasn't what he was after.

"This would be your job. I'll buy the plants, help you put them in, and I'll take what you pick to Gardella. Everything else is your job: staking, pruning, weeding, picking. It's your job for the whole summer. Pop will drop you off after chores in the morning, and I'll pick you and the tomatoes up in the afternoon. No milk routes. No dairy. Maybe a little haying, when Pop says so."

I nodded yes as soon as his last words made their way to me. For the whole summer, I was going to spend a couple of hours a day taking care of some tomato garden. Scratch and me, right next to the river! I was going to be able to fish all summer, and I was going to make enough to buy a car.

I did well until the tomatoes started ripening. In the early ripening, I could pick tomatoes up and down the rows with time to spare and fish for hours. Gradually, it took longer as more and more tomatoes ripened. Then one day, when my father came to get me, and we were loading up, he pointed to the far row. At first, I thought I might have missed a ripe tomato, but it wasn't so. A lot in that row and in some of the next were now ripe.

"You need to start picking twice a day."

In a few days, even that wasn't enough. I told my father.

"You're going to have to hire some help," he said.

"I don't have any money."

"Pay out of what Gardella gives us. Of course, that comes out of your share, not mine."

I told him this wasn't working out the way I thought it would.

"I guess you thought you'd caught yourself a good, one-sided deal."

My silence told him he was right.

He said that if I had told him the deal was too one-sided toward me, he would have told me why it wasn't. He had let me walk into a bad deal for myself.

"You can't cheat an honest man," he said. I knew what he meant, but I wasn't sure I believed it.

My first experience hiring people proved laughable. I hired my cousin Ronny for 25 cents an hour because he wanted less than Dick and John who demanded 50 cents. I showed Ronny how to look at the underside of the tomatoes for the "star." If the star was red, I told him he should pick it. One sullen hot morning I left him to start on the first row. When I came to bring him some water, I saw many of the tomatoes in his basket were dark green. When I compared a red star and a green star for him to see the difference, he confessed that he was red and green colorblind.

I can't know whether it was the dark dirt or just a good summer, but we grew more tomatoes than we ever thought we would. We had to buy more wicker baskets. Everyone, except the Boss, came up to Blood's land at the end of the day to help me pick. I tried to get Laura to help, but she said she didn't want to smell all over of tomatoes and have green hands like I did. At the end of one day's picking I found a jelly jar full of stones painted like tomatoes next to my picking baskets.

My father was pleased with how the summer had worked out. Driving home from our last trip to Gardella's, he grinned and said, "Remember this; I taught you everything you know, but not everything I know."

Don Crawford's garage didn't have any decent cars in my price range, so Uncle Carl sold me his Jeep for $50.

. . . .

Uncle Carl married his high school sweetheart, Rita. She was cute and loaded with energy. She learned to handle all the bookkeeping for the farm and took a real shine to Gypsy. She and Uncle Carl and some friends went Western dancing every Saturday night in a barnlike building in Attleboro. She invited me to go with them so many times that I finally said yes. Once she saw me dance, she never asked me along again.

Their first child was a boy they named Wayne. He looked just like Uncle Carl and was just as quiet. Wayne got known around soon as an adventurous kid. He felt no fear clinging atop a fully loaded, swaying, hay truck. We all liked to watch him scramble up the moving conveyor that carried bales to the hayloft where his fun was to ride up on a bale and then hang on and slide down with it into the loft. One summer afternoon, when the silo was empty, he had managed to drop himself down into it, but had no way to climb up the slimy walls. With the noise of the dairy and with Pop, Uncle Carl and me out haying, no one heard his yelling. Late that afternoon, after we brought the cows up and were getting ready for milking, we started to hear a hollow banging sound. The banging came in bursts, sometimes three bangs in a row, sometimes two, sometimes just one. We tracked the sound to the silo and looked down to see Wayne wielding a silage fork. We hauled him up and got the story, but his only real complaint was that he was thirsty.

Wayne's closest call came on a morning ride to his kindergarten a few miles down the state highway. The passenger door on the car he was riding in flew open when the car made the sharp left turn out of the farm drive, and Wayne tumbled out and rolled along onto the highway. No cars were near, and he simply popped up and got back in the car, and went off to Little Folk Farm as if nothing happened.

. . . .

Like most farmers around us, we kept a gravel pit far down back. It also made due as a dump for our broken and chipped milk bottles and trash like empty barrels and rusted-out machine scraps. A special wonder rested in our gravel dump: a 1930 Ford pick-up; battered, rusted gray-green, forsaken on its rims. Some days Laura and I would sit snug in it, have lunch, and imagine how we would fix it up when we got older and then we would have our own truck and drive anywhere we wanted. I mostly was for driving out west to go fishing. Laura said she wanted to head into Boston and drive all around to look at the store windows. She painted a rock with a picture of the truck.

I spent lazy hours rummaging through the bottles to find the ones that were just chipped, not broken, and set them up in front of the pit side and shoot at them. On the wall in the grain room, we kept a .22 long for shooting the woodchucks that dug holes that could break a cow's leg. Scratch hated even the sight of the .22, and the sound sent him in to keep company with Gypsy.

Laura was as good a shot as I was, and liked the deep *twhack* sound when she hit an empty bottle dead on. When I missed, and the bullet sent back a flinty scratch sound from the sandy gravel wall, Laura teased that I needed to go stand closer. My joke was to go stand closer to her.

One warm day, infused with aimless boredom, we took a break, tipped up an empty oil drum, and sat for lunch. The drum had been resealed with its screw cap.

"These things float, you know," Laura said. Our plan sprang out full-blown and all at once. We would build a raft.

We spent the next few days scouring our places for fence wire, baling twine, pulley rope, and anything that looked like it might be useful. My big find was an old double door off our root cellar that we had replaced with a new metal Bilco door. The old door was broken where the hinges had been, but still tight together otherwise.

Every day, we dragged our findings into the gravel pit, but except for the door and the barrels, nothing we found was of any use for the raft. By luck, I went looking for a hammer in the horse stalls and found all the old tack we had from back when we worked Tom and Jerry: harnesses, bridles, laces, and reins. Laura lashed it up and took it home where she dampened and dried the leather and loosened all their slip fittings. She furnished her authority to our raft building. The plan was that we would build the raft on the rock sled and use Gypsy to tow the sled to the river where we would slide it in.

In my last effort in the gravel pit, I used some old red primer to paint "Laura" across the deck. On the day of our first float, all went well getting from the gravel pit to the river. I unhitched the sled and turned Gypsy loose in the cow pasture. Scratch knew something was up and wouldn't leave my heels. When I came back, Laura had loaded us up with sandwiches and laid two fishing poles on the deck. She was beaming a smile, making her little motions with her hands, "This is going to be so great!"

We didn't need oars to move, but I figured we needed something to steer with, so I grabbed an old, long-handled shovel. Laura held on to Scratch, and I shoved us off. The whole thing barely floated, but hope was high. The river flow gradient was easy, and we spun once while I worked the shovel to hold us straight.

We stayed silent, content with being afloat. We turned our heads around and around, seeing things up from the river for the first time. She looped her hand over my back and sat alongside me.

"This is the best thing I've ever done," she said. "I want to do this every day."

A while later, we floated down to a cove where the river pushed almost no flow. We shared sandwiches with Scratch and sat, full up with our pride.

"Can we just stay here?" Laura asked.

"No anchor," I said. "Next time."

Drifting, now standing up, and wielding my shovel, I felt the raft begin to shift down. The barrels, already barely afloat, groaned and began twisting out of their leather harnesses. Laura propped to her knees, hands spread, and head up, eyes wide, looking at me. Scratch began to bark a frenzy, his rear haunches shivering from side to side. The raft pitched nose down, slopping everything into the river. I dropped the shovel. Scratch leapt for shore. A snap turn launched Laura's legs sideways, and she hit down full flat on her side, skidding across the wood door and into the water. I jumped in as close on top of her as I could reach as our whole contraption came apart under me. The raft barrels bobbed away slowly downstream while I thrashed around looking for Laura. I grabbed and grabbed at the blue denim shirt I could see moving below me. Scratch was on shore barking his lungs out, dashing first away from us then back again. I swam a few hard strokes, stabbed my arm down, and collected Laura around her waist. I knew we weren't in deep water and with a probe, I felt one foot tap bottom. Hopping and swimming, I hauled us in to shore. Laura coughed and choked and gasped in a big breath. She began to move and opened her eyes. In that second, my only thought was how small she was.

We made our way up from the river bank, scrambled over a stone wall, and pushed through a barricade of brush out into a pasture. "You OK?" I asked. She nodded yes. We stood there wet and torn up, more embarrassed by our building skill than injured by its failure. I heard Scratch bark and looked to see him on a dead run toward us, and behind him, long, strong legs pumping, came Charlie.

Charlie slowed to a trot, caught his breath, and looked us up and down. "I heard Scratch barking his head off down here and come to see that you've been taking a pretty sorry swim."

I let Laura tell him about our raft building and I confessed to its failure. Charlie told us to walk back to the gravel pit and dry off while he fetched back Gypsy and the rock sled.

At supper that night, Charlie didn't say a word about Laura and me and the raft, and the river never cared that we were there.

. . . .

"You know, the drivers are coming back with a lot more undelivered milk these days," one of the dairymen said to my father. My father called a meeting of the five drivers that afternoon.

"What's going on?" he asked

"Harry, it's cheaper at the stores. You know that," they all chimed.

"But it's easier for them to have it delivered," my father countered. "They don't have to go to the stores every couple of days."

Davy, the driver with the biggest route said, "They don't need to buy milk every couple of days. Everybody has refrigerators now. I had one woman tell me she wanted delivery only once a week to be sure she didn't run out."

That night, the Boss looked troubled. She had put together what the lower store prices, plus what the drivers had reported, could mean to us.

"This is a big change, and we have to set a compass about what to do."

It was like a crow over corn seed the way Grace Krill showed up in her gray Buick that next week. The Boss was standing outside watching how I weeded her glads. Grace didn't even get out of her car. She told the Boss about a small farm nearby toward Boston, one of the last ones, and that she and her family paid top dollar for it.

"Boston is emptying out. Development is moving this way. Just wanted you to know."

"I know what you wanted," the Boss said from where she stood.

Grace waved at me when she drove out.

. . . .

Charlie and I were sharpening saws in the small shed when we heard the Boss scream for Pop in a voice that echoed a boom off the dairy wall. We dropped our files and ran around the end of the barn up into the yard where we saw her shoulder to shoulder with Pop and Uncle Carl, pointing her cane at the barn.

"I saw him go in there," she said.

"Who," I asked, catching my breath.

She described a short young man in gray overalls.

"He was fiddling around over next to the pickup when I came out, and he ran in when he saw me."

Pop had told me we used to have our share of drifters during the Depression. "Mostly men looking for a quick handout and a place to sleep."

I had never seen one. Uncle Carl, Pop, Charlie, and I set out toward the barn and went in the big door, which was slid open for air while the cows were down in the pastures. I stepped to the right, into the grain room.

"The .22 is still on the wall," I said.

"Leave it there, but stay with it," Uncle Carl whispered.

Pop went behind the stations to the left, Uncle Carl to the right, and Charlie went down the main aisle of the barn. The three of them worked silently down the length of the barn. The far end of the mail aisle sat stacked with bales Charlie and I had thrown down from the loft. I watched Charlie halt and raise his arm.

"Hey!" he shouted. "I know you're back there. Come on out."

I grabbed the .22, tucked it under my right arm, barrel down, safety on, and stepped out into the main aisle behind Charlie.

Pop and Uncle Carl hustled back and gathered in the main aisle alongside Charlie, and watched as a young man – a boy – pushed his way out from behind the bales.

"He's a Lymie," Charlie said. Boys from the Lyman School were nicknamed "Lymies," and the boy's gray-ticking coveralls gave clear proof of his provenance.

I retreated to the grain room and put the .22 back on its pegs.

The boy's name was Rudy. He didn't know Charlie, but he had heard that Charlie was here at Hillcrest Farm and doing well. Rudy's plan called for him to find Charlie and see if he could work out some way to join him.

Two hours later, Rudy was in a two-toned blue state car headed back to the Lyman School.

. . . .

A Boston and Maine spur rail line ran through the north corner of the farm and crossed the river over the low, faded black trestle. I often walked the tracks to get to the trestle. I remained wrongly convinced that the deep water under the span held lots of fish even though I never caught one there. The dry, old railroad ties gave off a musty creosote smell, baking in the heat waves of the cinder rail bed. As I walked along the tracks, I always inspected the center of the ties where I could see, driven into each one, a numbered spike. The spikes carried one of five or six different numbers, and they appeared to follow no sequence. I invented an explanation that was perfectly acceptable to me: The spike number identified the team who laid that tie on the rail bed, and they hammered in the numbered rail spikes to get credit.

The trains ran only one way and didn't run on any real schedule that I could figure, but if I heard one coming, I raced to see it. I liked to count the cars and try to guess what was in them and where they were going. I knew they always slowed down going through the farm because of the cows, so one day when my cousin John was visiting, I dared him to sit on the railroad tracks with me while the train was coming and see who jumped away first. The engineer saw us a way off and blew the whistle. We just sat there. Of course, John jumped away first, and I stayed longer because I knew how slow the train moved. He told everyone at school I had a lot of guts because of how close the train came before I jumped off. But he told his mother who told my mother and I got scolded real good.

The Boss said I needed more than a scolding and told me to go cut a switch for a licking. It was the most scared I ever was, thinking for the whole time I searched after the switch about how much my licking was going to hurt. I cut a whippy branch from an apple tree and brought it to her in front of the dairy. She tossed it aside.

"Stand straight and still and listen to me. You need to think hard about everything you do around here. This is a farm where we all work and grown-ups can't be watching you all the time. You have to take care of yourself if you're to get on."

She made me stand there for a long time.

One day the train hauled a red caboose, and the man standing on the rail platform at the back waved to me.

. . . .

Everyone talked about one special train. It happened late one July day when I had gone down to the pasture gate to walk the cows up for milking. I had worked half the cows across the railroad tracks when I was startled by the train whistle. I closed the gate to hold back the cows that were still in the pasture and went after two cows wandering down the tracks. I got them back on the stone-walled path up to the barn and yelled for help. Charlie ran out to take care of the cows on the way up. I turned to cross back to rejoin the rest of the waiting cows in the pasture but the train was too close on me to make it across. The engineer blew three short blasts, I guess to make sure I wasn't going to try and cross. The train sounded different as it passed in front of me—loud, steady squealing wheels, groaning and clanking. I could feel the weight from the vibration through the ground. The train engine and coal car rumbled by, followed by several passenger cars, the kind we never saw on our tracks. I saw people inside, but none of them looked outside to see me. The next car told it all. It was a boxcar painted white, orange, and red with a figure of a girl standing, arms raised, in a ring of fire, and across the top arched in giant yellow words, "King Brothers Circus."

Car after car rolled by, all bending the rails with their weight. Scratch had been throwing some halfhearted barks at the train but picked up his pace at the next batch of cars. Some looked like cattle cars, but the bottom halves hung draped all around in cloth with bright paintings of clowns and elephants and other circus scenes. I thought I saw the head of a camel, but it turned out to be just a horse. I came up as close to the train as I could and imagined that I heard the roar of a lion. After the animal cars came flat cars loaded with disassembled parts for the rides: the Ferris wheel, the merry-go-round, and according to a red banner, "The Monster." It was the longest train that ever rolled through our farm. Every painted car excited me. I thrilled to imagine being part of the crowd inside the big tent with the clowns, the music, the lions, and the elephants.

After it had passed, and Scratch and I brought up the rest of the cows, Steve, one of our route drivers who had been standing with my family watching the train from the farmyard told me the circus had played Dennison Field in Framingham the day before. He asked why I hadn't gone to see it.

·················

Every kid in Framingham who went for the driver's license test knew two things: First, you were going to have to parallel park on steep Dennison Hill Road; then do a three-point turn to get down the hill all the while never getting your wheels on private property. Shifting gears, steering, and jumping from the clutch to the break, all the while on the steepest street in town, was accepted to be a genuine test of good driving. The second thing you knew was that you had to sign your driver's license before it was valid.

Bob drove me in the pickup to take my driving test. Before I went in to the Motor Vehicle office in the old Armory to take the written test, we went to Dennison Hill and I practiced parking and turning a few more times.

The written test was easy. The examiner walked me out to the pickup, and Bob got out and wished me good luck. To my surprise, we didn't go to Dennison Hill. We just drove back and forth across town in traffic. The examiner seemed to be interested mostly in how I gave hand signals for turns. When we finished, I drove back and pulled alongside the curb across from the Armory, a bit back from the corner. The examiner handed me my license and congratulated me. As he shut the door behind him, I reached for the pencil I had tucked in my shirt pocket, put the license on the seat, leaned down, and signed it. Smiling down at my signature, I put the truck in gear and eased off the clutch so I could move up to the corner. I felt a bump and looked up. I had hit the examiner who had chosen to cross the street in front of me. He stood and looked at me through the windshield, dropped his chin to his chest, raised it, and walked off to his office.

"How did the test go?" Bob asked.

"Fine," I said.

. . . .

I came up from getting wood shavings for the cows' stalls and saw the Boss pacing in the yard by the dairy loading docks, waiting for my father. She told me to find Uncle Carl and Pop and get everybody into the kitchen.

Calling everybody together in the middle of the day meant something big, and the Boss's scowl said it was bad news. I didn't like the looks of things. She had us stand around the blue-and-white, oilcloth-covered kitchen table.

"We're going to have to do something." She started out in a slow, steady voice, her eyes moving from the papers in front of her to us, to be sure we were listening. "The First National Stores called and told me this will be their last week with us. Just like A&P, they went with Sealtest. Customers buy cheaper at the store and buy only once a week now, and keep it in their refrigerators. No such thing as an iceman anymore. You can see we're getting more returns, and I can see that some customers are dropping us altogether."

Pop scraped his chair. Uncle Carl drew a glass of water.

"Now on top of that, we're making payments on credit, something we never did before." She reminded us that the new milk trucks, the new tractor, and the new dairy machines were all bought on credit. We were making ends meet but not by much, and she couldn't say for how long. Pop stared out the window toward the barn where his posse of cats lay about, carefree in the sun. My father and Uncle Carl ran their hands through their hair; a habit they shared. Both murmured that they needed time to think about it.

. . . .

More big changes kept happening over that winter. Traffic built up so much on Route 9 that they had to make it wider in some places and put in stoplights where it went through the dense shopping strip.

The stoplights turned out to be a good thing, because Huston Rawls, a developer from Boston, had an idea for a new kind of shopping center. His idea was to develop a shopping center especially for women shoppers who came by car. Downtown Framingham had poor parking and, worst of all, the busy rail lines ran right through the middle of town, cutting off traffic every time a train came through, stalling shoppers, and frustrating everybody. He chose 200 flat acres that had been Wyman's Garden Nursery for as long as anyone could remember. He called it Shoppers World, and my cousins and I went the day it opened in October 1951. The company bragged how the saucer-like dome over the Jordan Marsh store out in the front was the biggest one like it ever built. Two wings of stores stretched away from under the dome and bracketed a grassy courtyard park. Each wing had two floors crammed with all kinds of stores that carried names like Chandler's and Peck & Peck that we knew were from Boston.

Courtesy of Framingham History Center

For the first year, Shoppers' World was open, the company employed a corps of uniformed "Ask Me" girls who looked like stewardesses and walked around helping people find things. They even carried portable radios so they could tell people the score of the World Series games.

The most talked about thing, and the biggest reason we all went out there, was how the sidewalks on both floors could be closed off in glass from top to bottom, and you could walk around the whole place, indoors, in any kind of weather. The first year, my friends and I made special trips out during snowstorms. After a while, they got rid of the Ask Me girls and hired guards to make sure kids weren't hanging around the girls, getting in the way of real shoppers.

At the back of Shoppers World they added a movie theater called The Cinema. Even people who went to see movies in Boston said they had never seen anything so grand. I was getting sort of old for the Saturday matinees at the Hollis downtown, and I figured that Laura would like The Cinema.

Another movie theater opened not far from Shoppers World, the Natick Drive-In. When it first opened, we were glad to have a drive-in movie nearby instead of driving all the way to the old Shrewsbury drive-in near Worcester. We boys took our dates, both single and double dates, and hoped for romantic evenings.

However, the development along Route 9 now brought the Monticello (a big nightclub), Adventure (a drive-in restaurant), and more, and, unfortunately, all of it put a strain on the sewer system. The overloaded sewer beds lay open-aired right near the drive-in movie and the smell ruined any chances for a romantic evening. Laura said she would rather spread manure with me for three hours than sit through a movie at the Natick drive-in.

. . . .

No one in my family swore much, though I thought maybe Pop did when he spoke Swedish, so when I heard Uncle Carl swearing out in the dairy, I ran to see.

"Goddamn it!" he yelled and threw his black apron across the room. "A Goddamn crack." A stream of watery milk flowed across the floor to the main drain. I knew. We pasteurized our milk in giant glass-lined vats heated with hot water and you couldn't fix a crack. I was busting to say something to make him feel better but I hadn't learned those words. I picked up his apron and held it out. He put in on like he was asleep.

"Maybe this could be a good thing," Uncle Carl said at supper. We looked to him to tell us how a cracked vat could be a good thing. "The new way to pasteurize shoots the milk between stainless plates where the milk is on one side and steam, not hot water, is on the other side. What takes us hours now would take minutes."

"So why is that a good thing for us?" my father asked.

C. D. PETERSON

"Because with that extra open time, we could contract to pasteurize milk for small dairies like Echo farm and others as far away as Hudson and Shrewsbury and it wouldn't cost us much to add their extra milk in. We could charge them less than they could do it themselves."

The Boss laid her fork down. "The cost, though, Carl. How do we handle the cost? We could pick up a used vat somewhere for a good price."

Uncle Carl never liked being the center of things, and now we were all staring at him, forks in midair, waiting to hear his answer. He spilled it out slowly. "If we can bring in the new contract money from those smaller dairies, maybe we could afford to cut our prices to the big stores and get our business back. If we buy a used vat, we'll only be back where we are now."

It came to all of us, one at a time, sitting sad and poking at our plates; the problem was not going to sluice away. We that we had no choice but to buy the new steam pasteurizer.

Changes stirred up everywhere that winter. Pop tried to put Tom and Jerry down, but he couldn't do it, and called Simon from the slaughterhouse where we sent our bull calves. The heavy traffic now on Route 9 got Scratch the day after Christmas. They all said Scratch was old and wasn't going to last much longer, anyway. I understood life and death, but I had known Scratch all my life. I didn't know about this kind of death. It made me wonder what else I didn't know, what else could happen to me.

"You'll find out, *sot pojke*," Pop always said.

. . . .

I knew when serious snowstorms announced themselves. First, I could pick up a smell: cold, damp, sharp in my nose. Then it would begin, but not big, soft, lazy flakes floating to a puffy landing. No, the serious snowstorms threw down small flakes that hurried everywhere, darting in the wind with no time to waste. I watched them eager, swirling, as they searched for their place to join up and wait for the rest of the white hordes sweeping down from the sky. In no time, they erased brown and green and black. Like most kids, I got excited by snowstorms and the fun of sledding and skiing. But I knew that for every day taken off in the winter, it meant another day in school added on in June. Not even a whole week of winter snow fun was worth one day in June to me.

All of us spent the winter with dark doubts and troubled visions. It hit my father the hardest. He blamed himself for losing customers and for buying more trucks than we needed. He even blamed himself for the

90

cracked vat. He didn't like that my mother went to work even though the extra money helped. He didn't like that his boy had to work like a man. Pop told him that I hadn't been a boy since the war.

At least the snow that year gave us a break. After one big storm, we kept all the routes running and got to spread the manure plenty early, even on Blood's land.

....

Over the years, we used our sheds, pens, and coops to house all kinds of animals. Chickens and turkeys were regulars, but we often had ducks and once or twice we included Guinea hens. We always kept some pigs for slaughter at Thanksgiving and Christmas. More often than I liked, we raised sheep and goats. We kept only a few, and while they were smaller than cows, they took more work and attention and gave me more problems. Cows were docile for the most part, but our sheep and goats always produced one or two buck sheep or Billy goats that were just plain mean. One Billy we owned held a special dislike for me. When I went in the pen, it worked to get behind me and then make short charges, butting me on the back of my legs. If I turned and faced him, he would back away. I began to figure that if a dog could be afraid of the dark, a goat could be a coward.

My brother Ken was anything but a coward. One of the many chickens we raised was a very aggressive, barred rock rooster that ran loose in the yard. Ken was only two, playing in his sandbox, when the rooster went after him. I don't know how long the battle had been going on when I discovered it, because neither one of them was making a sound. The rooster would make a flying charge, and Ken, still sitting, would swing a wild punch at it. I ran the bird off and turned to see Ken with his two fists up like Joe Louis.

....

The business limped on a downward slope. We scoured for customers in the new housing developments where the boys poured their basements, then roofed and tar papered over them to live in until they could afford to build out. We did get some customers, but they didn't buy much. We hung on to local stores like Brockelman's, but we kept losing the big business in the chain stores that had now been ordered to buy on price. On top of that, the writing was on the wall that the small farmers who were paying us to pasteurize milk for them were facing the same problems we were facing, and they were not long for this world. We could see that the money we earned from them was going to dry up.

On the lookout for help, Uncle Carl spotted an article in *Farm Journal* magazine that told about a company that dairy farmers could hire to help them with problems.

"What do they know that we don't?" Pop asked Uncle Carl.

"Well, it wouldn't hurt to find out," he answered.

Pop and all of us agreed to have a man from Farm Services come and talk with us. Pop felt better when he met the man they sent, Bernhard Engman, and found that he spoke Swedish. Pop and Uncle Carl took Mr. Engman around on a walk of the farm: in the barn, by the tractor sheds, past the garages, and through the dairy. He spent the rest of the day in the kitchen talking with Pop, the Boss, and Uncle Carl. He said he would come back the next afternoon and tell us what he thought.

"You have a fine farm," Mr. Engman began, sitting at the kitchen table. "A first-class herd, well-maintained equipment, and a modern dairy with your new pasteurizer. You're some short on land, but what you farm is good soil with good yields. I'm sad to say I don't think I can make myself any money helping you," he said with a sad smile. "You're in a corner. You're not big enough to produce cheap milk, and you have no way to grow. Even if you wanted to get bigger and buy more land and cows, you would be up against everybody out there buying up land anywhere near Route 9 to put up stores and factories. And on top of all that, you already carry a big load of debt." He crossed his hands on the blue-and-white oilcloth. "*Jag ar ledsen,*" he said to Pop. "I'm sorry," he repeated to the rest of us.

"So what do you suggest we do?" The Boss asked.

Mr. Engman spoke in a deliberate, steady voice:

"You have a sound farm. Some small things could keep you going for quite a while." He nodded to Pop and said, "Keep on doing what you're doing to get new business, telling people why your milk is better." Then to my father, "Keep combing the new developments. If you can afford it, repaint your dark-blue trucks. Dark-blue is cold and somber. I'd paint them tan and cream, more like the golden Guernsey milk you're trying to sell."

He let his advice sink in.

He turned to the Boss, "The most important thing you can do is keep a lid on your costs." He spoke as though he was reading from a list. "Stop buying gas from the gas station across the street. Put in a gas tank of your own and buy gas cheaper in bulk. Don't buy new equipment if you can fix what you have."

Charlie, who had been fixing old equipment for months, smirked when he heard that. He dropped the smile when he heard what Mr. Engman said next, "If you don't have a full week's work for someone, let him go."

Again he addressed my father and suggested, "Combine your routes better. Your customers may not mind getting milk twice a week instead of every other day." We all nodded as he calmly laid out his ideas. "And change over from round bottles to square. Square bottles are cheaper and take up less space. Stores and home customers want that. Besides, in a few years from now, my company thinks that milk will be put up in special cardboard plastic cartons and that they will be square."

Mr. Engman looked around the table at all of us for some reaction. We mostly sat stunned. Finally, the Boss asked, "What do we owe you?"

He slid his bill over to her. "I wish I could have been more helpful. This is the second time this month I've had to deliver news like this."

Mr. Engman took Pop aside as we left the kitchen and said something to him in Swedish. Pop nodded sadly at what he heard.

Uncle Carl and the Boss sat and figured that by the end of the summer, we could run out of money. We were working in a daze.

. . . .

Perhaps because of the pressure, my father drifted into alcoholism. He was not the Jekyll and Hyde alcoholic, swinging from calm soberness to violent drunkenness. His basic, everyday nature was friendly and gentle. When he drank, he got sadly comical and then wound down into a quiet solitude, sometimes preceded by humming to himself or repeating some nonsense phrase. "Heading West in an open wagon," he once called up softly over and over, lying, eyes closed, on the couch.

At first, I didn't sense any seriousness to what I was seeing. My attempts to cheer him up were usually met with his pained smile. Soon, I came to understand, mostly from the Boss probing Pop or Uncle Carl with questions like, "How is he today?" or "Is he back yet?" that we were dealing with a deep problem. They talked about him "falling off the wagon."

He wanted my company and would ask me to go on his milk route with him. He knew I would rather work around the farm or go fishing, so he would scout me up out in the barn and make up reasons that he needed help: "My knee is acting up." "I have to deliver to the stores today."

If he really wanted me along, he would say that he planned to stop into Johnson's Hardware and look over the new fishing gear.

Everyone said he could drive better drunk than most people could drive sober, but I thought they were just trying to make themselves feel OK about it.

The Boss and Pop drew quiet during those times, exhausted with talks and threats. They were worried when I went with him as a striker. The Boss always gave me a dime and told me to telephone right away if I saw him drinking. I knew when he drank on the milk route. He would go into one of our restaurant customers and tell me to wait in the truck. He would spend a little more time in the restaurant than was right, and I could smell the drink on his breath. I never worked up the courage to say anything, but after his second restaurant stop, I would go silent and he knew. We would continue on with the route in a thin cloud of alcohol and mutual disappointment—I with him and he with himself.

One day, we were delivering milk in the Italian neighborhood near Lake Waushakum and stopped at a house with a grape arbor and where an old man named Mr. Brattica made his own wine. Mr. Brattica came out from the back of his house when we pulled in, carrying a gallon of shiny, purplish-red wine. My father got out of the truck and went to pay him, but I saw Mr. Brattica point to me in the truck and shake his head no and walk back behind his house. My father didn't argue; he just came back into the truck and we drove off. I could feel his shame and I hurt for him.

Again and again, I would tell myself that maybe this was the last time. I brimmed with a potion mix of hope and anxiety when he went for several days without a drink. "This is it. It's over." I was never angry when he faltered again; I knew it wasn't his fault. He didn't want to set his own life on fire like that. I hoped that the next time he stopped, it would last.

By the end of some routes, I did all the delivering, running up to houses and back. He would sit slumped in the truck and drive us to the next customer. I never did use the Boss's dime, though once I had to drive back to the farm when we finished. Just once. I never again doubted that I could find a way out of problems.

I knew the strain was building on my mother and father. The arguments were getting worse and harder to hide on the farm. My mother and my little brother, Ken, were spending almost all their time in town with her family. Although everybody tried to hide it from me, it was just a matter of time before divorce became a fact.

I hated the arguments more than anything; the sound of their anger and screaming. Their contorted faces frightened me and made me shake. I thought for a while that maybe I could have done something to prevent the fighting and the divorce, like threatening to run away. I made up fantasies about confronting them, giving them a deadline to stop, but as much as it pained me, I came to realize this wasn't about me. I could do nothing. My threat would be nothing more than pressing down on a spring, and as soon as I took the pressure off, the spring would pop back up again. I had my proof. Sometimes I would intentionally walk into a room when they were arguing; they would stop and pretend all was well, but as soon as I walked out, they would go at it again.

I came to figure this as one more thing, like the war or the weather, which I couldn't control. I would have to wait and find out. My parents had their own demons, born from the Depression and scarcity and nurtured on alcohol and too many easy choices after the war. They were left ill-prepared for abundance, and they vacated self-restraint. My mother and Ken took an apartment in town, and I divided my time between the apartment and the farm, but it worked out best for me to stay mostly on the farm. She worked two jobs, waitressing at night after her factory job. I worried about her health, but she said she had to make enough to take care of us. She was running ragged and spent too much time worrying about me, and so I worked to slip out from her care. I assured her she didn't have to worry so long as I was at the farm.

. . . .

My brother, Ken, was the nicest little boy I ever knew. Our six-year age difference gave us different lives early on, and he spent almost no time on the farm. When we were together in town, we often went to the backdoor of Barron's candy store where we bought leftover, broken milk chocolate in crisp, white bags for a dime. One afternoon, as we sat in the sun on the back steps of the store eating our chocolate, a well-dressed woman and her daughter approached to go in. We sat slightly in their way, and Ken and I heard the woman say to her daughter, "Just step around these ragamuffins." Ken jumped down and started to walk off. I stood and made them walk around me, staring at the daughter the whole time. Ken was hurt by the name-calling but, as was his nature, he got over it in minutes. (We talk about it to this day.)

Now that he lived in town, Ken started to visit the boy in the iron lung. When I asked him what he talked to the boy about he said, "He asks me questions about what I do every day and I tell him. His mother told me cries sometimes because he's lonely."

In time, my mother had a man friend, and we all assumed they would marry, and in time, they did. He was kind to her and Ken and considerate to me.

My father eventually got control over his drinking. He met a fine woman and friend who believed in him and over time, they married and had three lovely daughters. But my father's time on the farm was, in fits and stops, ending. With Uncle Carl's growing family—he now had two daughters, Gail and Lynn, to go along with his son, Wayne—my father felt that the farm couldn't support another person and that it was best if he move to Worcester and start his own milk delivery business. He was proud to take me on his routes and show me how successful he was in a very short time.

. . . .

Striking with the different route men delivering milk took me all over Framingham and the towns nearby. It was a perfect way to spot places to fish. One route into Southborough brushed by a narrow gap in the trees where I could glimpse the big reservoir hidden behind the dam. I had never fished there. One day I hitched a ride with a route driver and asked him to drop me off at the spot where I could see the reservoir. My plan was to walk in, fish my way back along the shore to the dam, and walk to the farm from there.

I started catching fish as soon as I threw my line in the water. They were all bass and all bigger than I usually caught behind the farm. I didn't want to lug them around all day, so I let them go as I caught them. I had brought a can of night crawlers, but I grabbed up crayfish out from under the rocks every chance I got. Fish hit the crayfish as soon as they landed in the water.

I picked my way along the stony shore at a good pace because I didn't know how long it would take to reach the dam. Late in the day, I finally spotted the dam and saw that I had a problem. I had figured that the shore would follow a straight line to the dam, but instead, the shore bent right and led out of sight. The reservoir was much larger than I'd thought. I'd walked too far to go back to where I came in, and I wasn't even sure I could locate that small gap. I couldn't keep walking along the shore; it could zig and zag a long way before rounding back toward the dam. My best bet was to strike off on a course to intercept the fire road and follow that back to the dam. I guessed, more than I chose, where to turn into the woods.

HOME FRONT

After a few steps, I knew I was in trouble. The woods along the reservoir had been planted thick with pine evergreens to protect the water from blowing leaves and dirt. Over the years, the undergrowth of bushes and vines had thickened into a chest-high wall. In places, I could manage only small steps, and then had to lean my whole weight forward to advance.

I had no watch, but as the light dimmed to a few bars of sunlight slanting through the thick woods, I figured it was probably chore time. Since I had begun spending time off and on with my mother in town, Charlie filled in for me without fuss, and surely would today when I didn't show.

I grew muscle tired, first pressing my chest into the brush and then hauling my feet up under me. If I tried to move faster, my feet got hooked in creeper vines and I pitched face forward into the sour tangle. I welcomed the thinned-out stretches where I could make some progress. I left my rod in one thin stretch thinking that if I wanted it – it was just another broken off radio antenna – I could come back for it.

I began to worry about getting turned around and walking in circles, but then I noticed that the pine trees had been planted in rows and spaced in a pattern. If I worked hard and kept my mind to it, I was able to follow the pattern and at least keep a straight path. My walking rhythm made a muffled, swishing sound, and sometimes I counted out my steps to myself. The trees had cut off what sunlight was left, but by sunset I'd sorted out the tree rows pretty well and the night left enough light for me to make my way. I counted my steps up to a hundred over and over, hoping I'd be out of the woods before I reached the next hundred. I stumbled out onto the dirt fire road well after dark; I guessed close to midnight.

It took a while to feel good—swinging long, easy steps, not worrying about getting caught up or falling. I collected my thoughts and took stock as I walked. I was scratched up, but I wasn't hurt. There was nothing in the woods to be afraid of. I was hungry, but I was used to going for long stretches without food when I went fishing.

Then I thought about everyone at home going crazy worrying about me, looking all over: the Boss clanging the barn bell and sending Charlie down to the deep trestle she feared so much; my father and Uncle Carl driving around my fishing spots; Pop with his flashlight searching the wells and pits; my mother telephoning Auntie Esther and Auntie Theresa, maybe even calling Laura or the state police.

I picked up my pace and set into a loping jog as fast as I could manage in the dark. I should have told someone I was going fishing. I was pained by what fears I was causing them. I had never gone missing, so I imagined how stunned they all must be, milling around, wondering, agonizing. I passed the dam and saw a dim light up in the control room. I cut across our hay field near Brewer's barn, aimed for the lights in the farmyard, and broke into a run as fast as I dared in the dark. My thudding feet were the only sounds.

I was sure to find a lot of activity and see the big house lit up with people moving around. I had rehearsed my story and my excuses for why it took so long to get home. But the yard was dead quiet. The usual yard lights glowed, but that was it. I slowly realized that no one would be worrying about me. My mother would think I was at the farm, and everyone at the farm would think I was at my mother's. I stood alone in the yard, figuring out what to do. Fatigue fell on me like a paralysis. I walked into the barn and fell on the hay.

No one was looking for me.

. . . .

Charlie McPhail left us, partly because he had become an extra on the payroll and partly because his car "borrowing" had gotten more brazen as he got older. The final blow came when a policeman came into our yard, and experienced in where to look, found a Lincoln hubcap on the cement apron behind the dairy – Charlie's usual trophy spot.

"Hello, Charlie," the policeman said, waving the hubcap at Charlie. "Last night someone took Mr. Al Franco's Lincoln from his house in Saxonville. When we found it, one hubcap was missing. I guessed I might find it here."

"I found that hubcap on my milk route, right along Central Street," I told the policeman. He knew I was covering for Charlie and knew there was nothing he could do about it. He put the hubcap in his cruiser, shot us a rueful smile, and eased down our gravel drive to Route 9.

Charlie wrote me a letter a month after he left us. He wrote from Florida, "Working around and having a good time." He wrote about how nice I had been to him, then he told me I needed to be careful because— he wrote in big letters underlined—YOU ARE NOT VERY SMART ABOUT ALL THE BAD PEOPLE OUT IN THE WORLD. I had a feeling he was right.

. . . .

I never saw a buzzard except in cowboy movies, but Grace Krill sure seemed to fit the bill, hovering over us. The Boss, tired as she was, always took care of Grace easy enough, running her off when she swooped by to tell us what she thought we ought to be doing. One day, she drove up while the Boss was out in the yard. She rolled down the window in the big Buick and spoke out to the Boss that we were getting pinned down by growth all around us; that Framingham wasn't a farm town anymore, that it was fast becoming a suburb.

"Harry's gone and Pop's not getting any younger," was Grace's out-the-car-window good-bye.

One steamy summer morning, Pop and I drove over to Brewer's hay field to gas up the small tractor and set Pop up to spend the day mowing and raking a first cutting of alfalfa. We went slow, carrying the gas can from the pickup, topping up the old machine, rechecking the hookup, and setting our pace for the hot day ahead. The sky lay milk white right on us. The air felt sullen and somehow "off." We completed our setup, and Pop started to climb on the tractor while I headed for the pickup. Then, from nowhere, we got knocked down flat by a flash of lightening and a clap of thunder right together on top of us. There was no storm, just the one flash and explosion in the haze. We stayed down on the ground to collect our wits, then Pop rose slowly, pushing up with one arm and grabbing the tractor with his other hand to pull himself up all the way. My ears were ringing. I rose first to my knees, then stood.

"What was that?" I asked.

"Heat lightening," Pop said, still straightening himself up. He climbed on the tractor and started it. I got in the pickup and drove back to the farm.

The air felt that same kind of "off" on June 6th, 1953. We seldom got morning thunderstorms in Massachusetts, but that morning small storms scudded by dropping quick rain bursts, and the air bristled. The sun came out, but the wind blew like we were in a storm. During the day, the sky took on a hazy blur of yellowish tan. Black clouds formed, but barely held together, falling apart as they blew by. For hours, roaring gusts were followed by dead calm. As we passed each other working, we exchanged looks of bafflement and confusion. Midafternoon, the Boss sent me to go collect up some new milk bottles from our storage shed in Fayville and to get back before chores. During the ten-minute drive on the small roads to Fayville, I heard the air crackle and wheeze.

While I was loading the bottles at the storage shed, I looked up and saw leaves and branches swimming around, high in the sky. When I drove back into the farmyard, Pop, the Boss, and Uncle Carl were standing there watching the sky. One of them and then another would point. When

I joined them, I saw that they were pointing at things: shingles, small boards, and trash, all turning slowly, high above us. I bumped into Pop as we shuffled around the yard, gaping up at the yellowing sky.

"Jesus," Uncle Carl said. The Boss grabbed at his sleeve. "I've never seen such a sight in my life," she said.

An earth- shaking thunderstorm hung over us during chore time, and rain flooded the farmyard. Then the sky swept clear, the wind died, and the air rinsed out. At supper, the phone rang again and again with people calling us about the tornado that hit Worcester and killed nearly a hundred people. I called Laura but her phone was out. After supper, Uncle Carl and Pop went all around the farm to see what damage we might have. When they came back in, the Boss, sitting at the kitchen table, looked shaken as she told them, "I heard on the radio the tornado hit Brookside Farm, killed six of their men and all eighty cows." We realized how lucky we had been.

I drove over to Brewer's barn. The dirt road was filled with tree limbs that I had to haul aside. The barn looked fine when I got there, but trash lay all over. I tried to drive to Fayville to check our storage shed, but I found the State Police set up in a roadblock. I saw old Mr. Brewer standing and talking with the troopers. He waved me over.

"Fayville's been tore up," he said. "The tornado touched down at the post office. Crushed three people." The Boss heard later that two of the people crushed were Mrs. Noborini, a nice German lady who married an American soldier, and her one year old son. They were milk customer of ours.

Pop didn't find much damage around the barn and sheds, but Uncle Carl had hiked down into a couple of our hay fields and found them full of trash, mostly roof shingles and wood shards. Around a quiet dinner, Uncle Carl told us how we faced a tough summer mowing.

"If any of that junk with shingle tar and roofing nails gets to the cows, it can kill them. We can hardly hand scythe the whole place. It'll be damn slow going with the mowers."

Pop nodded and said, "The hay's ready to cut now. We'll see how bad it is as soon as it's dry enough."

The hay was tall enough to hide the trash until we got close up to it. We worked to hand pick the fields clear by driving our big, flatbed truck into a few central spots and carting the trash to it. The truck had only slat sides so stuff could blow or fall off. We used the pickup, too, but it didn't hold all that much. We got way behind on mowing, and when we did mow, the trash we missed – cardboard boxes, shingles, branches - jammed the sickle blades. We even found a hubcap Charlie would have liked. After the second day of mowing, I found Uncle Carl in our repair shed replacing a whole sickle bar.

"Some poor soul's window frame jammed under a blade and busted the whole bar," he said, nodding to a chunk of white-painted wood on the dirt floor next to the mower.

We worried about baling up trash with the hay, so after we cut and raked the hay, we patrolled the acres of windrows slowly, looking for anything we missed. We still ended up baling some trash and threw part of the first cutting into the gravel pit dump. When we got ready to use the hay, we stayed careful to shake it out when we fed the cows, and no harm ever did come to the cows. The tornado caused a lot of extra work for us and cost us time and money.

"We didn't need this," Pop said.

. . . .

Development surged everywhere. Along Route 9, new restaurants and nightclubs drew people out from Boston. Ken's Steakhouse, a milk customer of ours, had so much new business that they doubled the size of their restaurant. The singer, Vaughn Monroe, built a supper club called The Meadows where he broadcast his radio show.

Returning veterans, helped by VA loans, opened businesses around the industrial parts of South Framingham. They grabbed opportunities in the housing boom and the new General Motors plant. Some of the veterans set up their machine shops and small factories in metal Quonset huts that the government was selling for almost nothing to get rid of them. A few veterans bought Quonset huts and turned them into their homes.

Some of the boys caught on to a fresh business idea. The new television sets weren't all that reliable and often needed repair. Some vets had learned about electronics and electrical repair while they were in the service. Now, they needed only a few special devices to open TV and radio repair shops, many right from their homes. I delivered milk to Eddie Trudel who had his TV repair shop in his garage.

"How's business," I always asked.

"I need another wood pallet. I got so many broken sets coming in. I have to keep them off the ground. Plus, I need some place to put my parts."

I told him I would bring a pallet next time.

"Bring me some help, too. I have to go in the antenna business now. People think there's something wrong with their TV, but it's the dammed rabbit ears, so when they find that out, they want me to put up an antenna. Easy money, but already I need maybe two guys."

I told Eddie we needed help, too. We agreed things were tough these days. Eddie took out his comb and glided it through his now re-grown thick black hair, stuck the comb back in his pocket and waved me away.

"Help Wanted" signs decorated store windows and draped telephone poles.

We were not the only farm to have trouble hiring help. Avery Thompson, a vegetable farmer north of us, came up with the idea of bringing in workers from Puerto Rico. He came to see Pop about it. They leaned against Mr. Thompson's big flatbed.

"I got all this work, runs only spring to fall, ten hours a day, then nothing. Kids don't get out of school until June, and their folks don't want them pulling weeds ten hours a day six days a week. So, I read that a farmer in New York brings in Puerto Ricans for the summer. I called him up, and he told me Puerto Rico is like a state now, so people from there can come here without a passport or special papers. I went to see a man in Boston who sets it up."

"How many are you bringing?" Pop asked.

"Ten to start. I'll let you know how it goes."

Thompson's Puerto Rican workers became a novelty in their bright, white shirts that stood out when they came into town and idled away Sundays in front of the Wellworth restaurant and St. George Theater. My friend Bobby Cox and I would nod and say hello and slow down to see if we could get a conversation going, but they just smiled and looked at their feet. They did not flirt with the girls, though I think some of the girls wished they did. Laura told me that some of the girls thought the workers were dangerous and exciting. Art Fitzgerald, an usher at the St. George, told everyone that the Puerto Ricans all carried knives.

Mr. Thompson grew his crew from ten workers to twenty. Their presence downtown spread, but people felt comfortable knowing that the Puerto Ricans would be gone when the leaves fell.

At first, the workers did return to Puerto Rico at the end of the season, but after only a few years, they started to winter over, renting rooms in the south of town. Pretty soon, more Puerto Ricans came, and not all came to work on Thompson's farm. Everybody needed help, so they slid into jobs here and there. An old, blue school bus gathered up workers every morning in Irving Square and drove into Boston, dropping off workers as it went and returning them at night.

The newcomers opened small stores and restaurants to serve themselves. Mr. Johnson at the hardware store said, "Framingham will never be the same. These people will take over, you'll see."

I asked Pop if we would hire any Puerto Ricans.

"I hardly learned English; I'm not going to try to learn Spanish."

I marked Thompson's venture as one more transformation after the war.

Only years later did I realize how profound a change this seasonal shortage of workers made in everyone's lives.

....

Three of the seasons—spring, summer, and fall—edged up on us a bit at a time. Spring sent us a signal in early March when the temperature bumped up to shirt-sleeve warm. Passing each other, working, we smiled in silent agreement of how good it felt. The sun etched high-slanted rays into the last of the grainy snow piles hiding out behind the barn, and shrunk away the last of the anchor ice on the edge of the river. We usually got knocked back into some deep cold, or a snowstorm, but it didn't last, and we knew from that early day winter had begun to soften into spring.

Spring arrived at a sly leisure, but built into a crescendo. A few lonely sentinels of green poked up here and there, waiting. Then a few buds pinked. Morning's frosty ground melted to mud by midday. On the milk routes, I could see crocuses and daffodils coloring the warmer spots and sunny hillsides. Then, in a rush, apple blossoms, dandelions, and our big lilacs with their foot carpets of violets showed themselves full.

Summer slid in on us with an exquisite, steady persistence. Green overran everything. It leafed out bare trees, spread over low spots, and engulfed the brown briars that had played dead for months. Vernal pools shrank in their seasonal retreat. We rushed to keep ahead of it with our plowing, harrowing, and seeding, but in no time everything stood drenched in shades of green.

Once on us, it seemed summer would last steady and forever, growing and mowing and growing again. Hot days and more, endless, hotter days, raking and baling. And always fishing—in the coves, by the rocks, below the dam, at Raceland, near the lily pads—everywhere. But then, sometime beyond mid-August, I would sense it, always in the still, noon of the day, maybe while I was fishing or taking a break standing in a field. I could sense the universe come to a halt, and in that pause, the earth would breathe a long sigh. I felt a flash of chilliness from the silent sun, even though the deep shadows nearby preserved calm, green warmth. No sound, no breeze, no stirring signaled, but I knew before anyone that the summer had just given consent to autumn's will.

Autumn played us coy, shading the green leaves with a sneaky hint of bronze in September, maybe hoping we wouldn't notice. Soon enough though, bright reds and golds shouted the season. Spicy smells erupted when I walked through our meadows. Mr. Brewer's orchards now grew pungent with cidery smells from squashy, fallen apples that he no longer had workers to help pick. Though Laura and I tried to help, harvesting apples meant lots of people picking in a short span of days. He got some weekend help, but most everybody, even high school kids, had jobs now. The rotting fruit brought swarms of bees and two families of deer.

Most autumns faked early death. They hit with a bristling frost and a night cold enough to ice over the bull pen water trough, but then they resurrected themselves into summerlike warmth. After autumn's deceit, Indian summer buzzed along, modestly shrinking each cooler day and lengthening the chillier nights, mostly unnoticed.

Unlike the rest, winter crafted no pretense. It did not arrive gently nor play coy with us. Winter claimed its place from its first, cold, windy, raw day, and wouldn't give it up for months. In fact, once started, it would pour it on, pointing out every door Pop had failed to snug, every window I missed caulking, and every truck battery Uncle Carl had nursed for too long. Winter sun, at its best, sat in the sky like a pale poker chip over the bones of our fields and stone walls.

Each winter brought its own personality, and perhaps because we were starved for goings on, we kept the subject of our winters as the center of constant conversation. We detailed to each other every notable low temperature, counted up the successive days of gloom, and secretly cheered on each snowfall to break records. We compared this one to that one, and Pop would top all our talk by boasting about some cruel winter years ago in Sweden.

. . . .

We kept our calves and heifers pastured out during the summer. They mostly got on well enough grazing, but they needed grain, and in dry times, even some hay. The spot we used for feeding them sat at a gate off shady Brewer Road to the river. Over the summer, I spilled a good bit of grain around the gate, and that attracted pheasants and other wild birds, which would scatter out of my way when I drove up at feeding time.

I never hunted, except for shooting woodchucks—and that was a job, not a sport—but some of the boys at school liked hunting. Lee, the captain of the football team, and Harry, our star hockey player, once asked me if I ever saw any pheasant on the farm. Lee and Harry were very popular, and though they said hello, nodded at me, and talked to me once in a while, we weren't really friends. I figured they saw me as a farm kid, just someone in the background.

"Oh, I see lots of pheasants. We feed grain to some calves down off a dirt road, and I scatter birds all the time."

Lee asked if they could come out and hunt when pheasant season opened. We had our calves and heifers back in Brewer's barn by then, so I said OK.

The Monday after hunting season opened, I saw Lee in the hall at school and asked how he and Harry made out hunting.

"We saw one pheasant and Harry missed the shot. It looked like a perfect place, on the edge of a field with scattered grain around. We stayed for a while, but never saw another bird."

I said how it was too bad, and he said thanks, anyway.

When I told my father about it, he said that pheasants and deer knew exactly when hunting season opened and knew to go into hiding.

While hunting held no interest for me, but I spent hours hanging around Johnson's Hardware where Mr. Johnson was only too happy to talk fishing with me. I admired the five-pound, brown trout mounted on a plaque above the fishing counter. He said he caught it in New Hampshire, but I wasn't sure he did because he said he forgot the name of the river.

Mostly I bought small white tins of assorted hooks and a new line once in a while, but one day I decided to look at buying a new rod. He had steel True Temper rods that you could make the tip touch the handle and not break it, but they were a few dollars more than I could spend. The prettiest rods in the rack glowed golden warm and had fine-green thread wraps around the guides. Some handles were cork, but some were burled rosewood. The rods weren't round, they were hexagonal. I asked Mr. Johnson about them.

"Those are bamboo fly rods, 'cane' some people call them." He took a Heddon #10 out and let me handle it. "To make a rod like this you need to treat the bamboo, slice it into long tapered strips just so, and glue them together. Then you need to finish it and not leave one mark in the varnish. The guide eyes are agate inside so the line will slip through real smooth. Some fellas earn a living making the fancy rosewood handles."

I swished the rod back and forth and it felt alive. I said so to Mr. Johnson.

"That's because it once was alive," he said. "It will give you slow, smooth casts. You can't hurry a cast or flip a fly here and there. That bamboo rod will do what's in its nature to do."

The bamboo rod cost thirty-five dollars. I settled for a five-dollar fiberglass rod.

. . . .

I never saw the Boss, Pop, or my father, go to a movie, a restaurant, or a ball game. Uncle Carl and my Aunt Rita did go out dancing once a week, and my mother went to the movies Thursdays with her sisters to get the sets of dishes, but that made up about all the outside entertainment they did. The Saturday matinees and some of our magazines gave me a glimpse of how other people lived in places like Hollywood, but I bet those were fantasies. Later, television opened my eyes and created self-doubt about how much I really knew.

Somehow, I thought I would come to understand more and sort of grow into the adult world. I watched kids a few years ahead of me get older, graduate, get jobs, go to college, get married, or enlist in the service. They glided easily into being adults.

Then things changed. In my first year of high school, only a few senior boys had cars, and if you were a pretty girl or had cigarettes to trade, you could get a ride to Sunshine Dairy Ice Cream or to a Saturday football game. By the time I became a senior, though, so many boys and girls had cars that kids came late for class because they had to park far away. After school looked and sounded like the Eastern States Exposition, with bunches of kids running to cars and with engines all roaring to life at once. The new thing to do was to just drive around to see the sights and to be seen. Kids had never been able to do such things before, and they acted giddy owning this new independence. Our parents didn't seem to notice because they were busy exploring their own new lives.

The cars came first, and the music came next. Some kids listened to a new music called rhythm and blues; "black music" some called it. It sounded strange to me, but I came to like it. For a long while, everybody sang a song called "Sh-Boom" by a white group. I thought it OK and sang along because all the kids did.

A final, big change came from the movies. It seemed to me that up until then, movies were either for adults or children. Other than cheap horror movies, none were made for kids our age. Things changed that year with two movies. First came, *Blackboard Jungle*, a story about a tough high school in a city slum. It posed surly, high school kids talking back to teachers and bullying adults. The match to the gasoline that lit kids off was the song, "Rock Around the Clock." Kids now called the music "rock 'n roll." It belonged to us. Boys bought leather jackets and mimicked the swagger of the kids in the movies, while the girls, when they could get away with it, smoked in public.

Suddenly, we became a special group. A new radio station, WKOX, came to Framingham and one afternoon a week someone from our school became the announcer. All week long, we could hear our names being called out for dedications. The station broadcast our Saturday football games.

Television and the magazines started labeling us "teen agers," a new, awkward idea to everyone. The idea fashioned a very fast rebellion, and lots of kids got recruited by a second movie, *Rebel Without a Cause*.

My usual anxiety about time took on a new feel. As a child, I felt I could stretch out time by making sure I didn't waste a minute. My mother laughed at my crude schedules and how I left the pages of the calendar unturned. Now, our money problems and work on the farm took on steady background cadence, but when I started my senior year in high school, time began to feel like some heavy river flow carrying me along.

We all drove around, full of laughter, everything was open, we were at peace, there were jobs everywhere, polio had been cured, and we had our new music. We felt special and powerful. Everything seemed to be moving at new, double time.

No one else seemed to be aware that everything that was happening was temporary. But I could tell, so strongly, that our lives were flying on the way to something nameless and soon all this would be gone. When I tried to talk to Billy or Bobby about it, to ask them if they felt it too, they would tell me that I was too serious, like everyone said. They told me that was why people went quiet when I came around. Laura said that my problem was all because I spent too much time pondering things I didn't understand.

. . . .

My friend, Billy Dyan, owned a great car, a sand-colored 1948 Mercury convertible. One summer Saturday, we decided to prepare for our night's double date by cleaning up his car, inside and out. We washed and waxed it, scrubbed the whitewall tires, and cleaned all the stains on the horse-hair cloth seats. That night, as we drove to get Laura, I started to feel a burn on my rear end. I shifted my position a few times. then lifted up and slid my hand underneath myself. Billy also started squirming.

"You feel something hot?" Billy asked. I nodded, and he pulled over to the side of the road. "My ass felt like we were on fire," he said, crouching to look under the car. We put our hands on the seats and could feel the heat. With the car stopped and our heads bent in, we could smell the solvent we had used to clean the seats.

We decided to use the floor mats to sit on until we got to Laura's where we could figure out what to do. Laura and Mr. Rawlings had a big laugh when we explained things. Laura went and dug out two horse blankets, and she and Billy and I all gave a test sitting. Mr. Rawlings just sat on his porch laughing. He said we could use his old pickup, but that meant that one couple would need to ride in the back, and he couldn't guarantee what had been hauled back there was any better than what Billy and I had used to clean the seats.

We were glad Billy's date went to Milford High School so that the story wouldn't get around Framingham. Laura said she wouldn't tell anyone how dumb we were because she didn't want to hear any hot-ass jokes.

We all broke our vow of silence right before graduation, and we lasted through a week or two of hot-ass jokes just fine.

. . . .

As things began to tighten, my father and I looked for ways to earn extra money. Short-handed, we didn't have the time to raise tomatoes again, so my father decided to follow around after our milk routes on Thursday afternoons and sell eggs. He had my brother Ken and me help him. I hated knocking on doors and asking people to buy eggs, but Ken was a cute kid and took to selling right away. Pretty soon, my father said I could skip the egg route.

I recognized the money to be made in selling and figured out a way to make money without knocking on doors. We planted a lot of cow corn for silage, and we also kept a patch of sweet corn for ourselves. The Boss had her own way of cooking corn. She got the water boiling on the stove and, only then, had me go pick and husk a dozen or so ears. She'd rush to drop the corn and a few husks into the boiling water for a few minutes cooking. "The sooner off the stalk you can cook the corn, the sweeter it is"

The difference between sweet corn and cow corn was that cow corn grew in bigger ears and had larger, starchy kernels. I knew from my cousins that peddlers selling vegetables drove into the Italian and Portuguese neighborhoods, parked, and called to people to come out and buy. When buyers stopped coming out, the peddlers moved to another part of the neighborhood until they sold out.

I loaded the pickup with ten or so grain sacks of sweet corn and drove into the Italian section of town early one Friday afternoon. I had to call out only once or twice before I had customers lined up. It took me five stops, the last one in the Portuguese neighborhood, to sell out. At four in the afternoon, I had to rush to get back for chores, but I was able to lay almost twenty-five dollars on the big round kitchen table. It would have been more, but I had bought a loaf of warm bread from Cavagni's and a cold lemon ice from Lapenta's.

The next Friday, I didn't have enough sweet corn to fill ten bags, so I filled the last three or four with cow corn. I started in the Portuguese section.

"You back again? Good!" a woman said. She stood back as I dumped one bag of sweet corn and one bag of the larger cow corn out onto the bed of the pickup.

"There you go," I said. "Pick what you want." By now two other women were at the truck. To my surprise, they all grabbed for the large corn. Smiling, one woman held an ear of the large corn up to me shaking it, "Grande de mehlo," she said and stuffed the ear into her own bag. I was surprised, but clearly that's what they preferred. In the Italian neighborhoods, people would take either one, and I sold out again.

By the time the corn season ended, I had brought in more money working one day a week picking and selling corn than I did working all summer raising tomatoes. Unfortunately, it brought in too little, too late to do much good.

. . . .

Our need to bring in more income ran straight into a dream my father harbored for years: he wanted an ice cream stand, one that served hot dogs and hamburgers. He was sure that being right out on Route 9 it would attract lots of customers. Plus, we could count on our milk customers to come out.

What I took to be a small undertaking turned out to be a much different project. It began with a full cement block basement and a ground level walk-out door. Because my mother was Italian, they all teased that I should be the chief block layer. They offered no reasoning as to why I should be the carpenter's helper or the plumber's associate or general gofer, but there I was. The 'stand' became a three story building with the basement for storage, the main floor for the operations, and the top floor held open for, what my father imagined would be, a person to run the place.

We installed top flight equipment and bought only first rate supplies. A big road side sign announced our opening, as did the flyers that our drivers dropped off with deliveries to our milk customers. At first we had lots of people come out. We began to think we had found a way out of our money problems. But we came to realize how that first flood of business came mostly from curiosity seekers. Soon a pattern developed where we were crowded on weekends, but had little business during the week. The stand sat at the farthest west edge of town, while business – and traffic – was developing around Shoppers World, miles away at the eastern edge. Kids from school came out once in a while, but the new attraction for them now was a big drive-in car hop called Adventure.

We had no rent to pay and the business we took in covered costs, so we hung on thinking we might be able to sell it.

....

When I saw Uncle Carl driving out in the field toward me in the middle of the day, my jaw tightened. I stood stock still watching how long he took to open the door and get out. He small talked about how the fields looked dried out, pretending to look up and down the piece. I waited.

Finally, "What if we sold out to Houghton?"

He saw me deadpanned, waiting for him to say more. He explained how he thought that we would be a good buy for the big dairy; how our business was all set up—new pasteurizer, new tractor, new trucks. They could step in and we step out.

When I asked if the Boss and Pop knew about this, he said no; he wanted to ask me first what I thought. He went over it again, telling how it was getting tough for us. He had three kids now. Pop was getting older, and I needed to be thinking about what was ahead for me. I walked to the truck and leaned on the fender with my hands. I saw it was killing Uncle Carl to talk to me. His eyes twitched, and he ran his hand through his hair every few minutes. His hair had thinned. and I wondered when that started happening and why I hadn't noticed before.

As much as I hated it, the picture came clear: with all the changes and development, we had no way to grow and keep up. We couldn't afford to buy land, and we couldn't hire help at what factories were paying. As proud as we felt when the newspaper showed that our "registered golden Guernsey" milk was the finest, people wouldn't pay extra for it. Our land had become worth too much to farm it.

I asked him when he planned to tell the Boss and Pop. He explained that his plan was to keep from upsetting them until he knew how good a deal we could get from Houghton. His idea was to meet with Henry Houghton and get a notion of what they might pay; he wouldn't promise Henry anything. I told him I didn't like doing this behind the Boss's and Pop's backs. Of course, he didn't either, but did I have any other ideas? I didn't, and Uncle Carl started for his truck.

I asked to his back, "What would we do if we sold?"

He looked away across the field when he turned to answer.

"The money will let the Boss and Pop take it easy down Maine, for sure. Your parents are doing fine on their own, and I always have jobs waiting for me at Moline or John Deere. Lots less work and lots more money," he said.

After an awkward pause, he added, "There'd be money for you to go to school."

I went fishing to stall going back. The water lay smooth and silver perfect. Under overhanging branches, I saw caddis flies buzzing and bouncing on the water like drunks. Blue damsel flies swooped and darted, thin and graceful. A fish finned in the current just below the surface. In a slow rhythm, it lifted its head every few seconds, barely enough to grab a caddis floating by. I decided to sit and watch it.

Uncle Carl stood near the garages waiting for me. I asked about the meeting with Henry Houghton. He shook his head. "No meeting. I had trouble even getting him on the phone." When Henry finally came on, he told Uncle Carl he wasn't in the cow shit and tractor business anymore, but he might want our dairy and the milk routes.

"What now?" I asked.

A week later, Henry Houghton had his lawyer call to say they had no interest in buying our dairy business. He said they would probably send someone to bid on the milk trucks if we held an auction.

That night at supper, I could see Uncle Carl making nervous stabs at his food, and finally he clinked his fork down against his plate and cleared his throat. "I called Henry Houghton and talked to him about buying out our business."

Silence.

"We can't stay with this, and I figured if Houghton bought the business and the Krills bought the land, we might come out OK."

Pop raised his head and looked toward the ceiling. The Boss sat stone faced for a bit and then asked, "What did Henry Houghton say?"

"He had his man call to tell us they might come and bid on the new Divco trucks if we had an auction. That's all."

We poked around, halfhearted, at a few ideas about what to do, but in the end, we decided that the Boss would call Grace Krill in the morning.

I didn't sit in on the talks between the Boss and Grace Krill. About a week on, Grace pulled up behind me while I was gassing up at Crawford's. She got out of her car and walked over to me.

"I'm trying to make it plain to your grandmother that your place is just some pastureland and a rocky hill. I can't get that many good building lots out of it. You'd be smart to tell her I'm right."

She wasn't expecting an answer from me, so I just nodded that I'd heard her, buttoned up my gas tank, and drove off.

. . . .

"Seems to me you sure are on-again off-again with Laura Rawlings," Charlie said to me one evening watching me climb into the pick-up. He saw it right. Sometimes she and I would go weeks as thick as thieves and then, for no reason, one of us would back away. When that happened, neither of us questioned why, I suspect because neither of us had an answer. Then, in a few days or a few weeks, one of us would make the move to join up again like nothing happened. I came to expect the together-apart cycle of it, though I didn't like it much, and Laura seemed to expect it, too. I can hardly say why, but somehow it felt as though we were practicing.

. . . .

From the beginning, boys and girls from farms understood they couldn't go to someone's house after school because of chores. It was hard to be on a sports team. We got invited to parties sometimes, but we were never part of things like neighborhood gangs or kick-the-can games. We mixed at Saturday matinees at the Hollis and Fourth of July fireworks and by watching the marathon go through town, but we were different. Being different seemed pretty natural and harmless to me. In my senior year of high school, I got called to the assistant principal's office and found out it wasn't natural at all, and it certainly wasn't harmless.

Every kid feared being called to our assistant principal's office. My call to see him came soon after Christmas break. Mr. Ralph Martin looked harsh, sounded harsh, and handed out harsh punishment, so I was surprised at how friendly he welcomed me when I walked in. He smiled and acted nervous when he introduced me to a rumpled, white-haired man he called a guidance counselor. We sat at a round table.

He put his hand on a folder lying on the table and said, "I think we owe you an apology, Douglas."

The next few minutes changed my life.

Mr. Martin was sure I knew that students took different kinds of classes going through school. We all knew there were college kids, vocational kids, and the rest of us working and farm kids. Mr. Martin told me that they had put me on the wrong track. A special state education test we all took back in September showed me at the top in everything. He kept clearing his throat and said how they should have been preparing me with college courses and now we were halfway through my senior year. I learned on the spot that people I thought were smart could be wrong.

He and the guidance counselor had been working to see what they could do.

I told them we couldn't afford college anyway, and I was probably going to join the navy. They persisted, insisting that ways could be found. Mr. Martin opened the folder and slid a brochure across the desk.

"You still have time to apply for an NROTC scholarship. Four years paid tuition and books, plus a monthly stipend, in exchange for four years serving in the navy as an officer."

The timing was tight, but I could make a sitting for an all-day NROTC test scheduled in a week in Boston. If I passed the test, I would be called to an interview with the navy. Mr. Martin told me he had found out that some colleges held slots open, even this late, for late NROTC applicants because they trusted the navy's tough screening and welcomed the scholarship money.

A week later, I drove my half-heated Jeep in a fair snowstorm to the Navy building at100 Milk Street in Boston. The front doors opened into a large lobby with four reception desks, but only one was manned. I handed my letter to the sailor in a blue uniform sitting behind the desk. He studied it a while, then told me to go down the first hallway to the room at the end. The walls were milky white with a chest-high blue stripe. I thought at first that the gray linoleum floors were wet, but they were just shiny. The occasional sailor walking by me in the hall echoed clicking noises with each step, the shoes below their bellbottom pants gleaming black. I passed by several completely empty offices. The offices that were open were noiseless, with a few sailors scattered quietly behind gray steel desks. I imagined what this huge place was like a few years before, during the war.

I pushed open a metal door and found the large, empty room set up classroom style. I took a seat, and in a few minutes, a sailor came in and motioned me to come forward. He handed me a folder and some pencils. He explained that this was a makeup test and that I was the only one who would be taking it since the others had canceled because of the snow. I was allowed two hours for the first unit, and then I would have a break with a box lunch at my desk. The second session had no time limit, and I could leave when I finished.

The first test session contained mostly multiple choice, a lot of them word–math questions. I felt I did OK. The second session was unlike any test I had ever seen. Each page presented three or four paragraphs of complicated information about some subject: a medical condition, a business situation, a historical event, and so on. Then I had to write out answers to several questions about the subject. I felt like it was an open-book exam. I cruised through it in an hour. I waited a few minutes for the sailor giving the test, who had looked in on me every once in a while, to poke his head in. When he came and collected my tests, he questioned whether I was certain that I had answered all the questions. I told him I was certain, and he took my folder.

Driving home, I imagined myself as a navy pilot flying in a snowstorm.

....

The screen door slapped, and the Boss came out into the yard, now leaning on her cane, with the letter from the Navy Department held high so I could see it from where I stood by the tractor shed. She watched as I tore it open and learned that I was scheduled for an interview because of "the superior results of your written examination."

My family, overjoyed and thankful, wanted to support me, but this was all new to them, too. No one had been to college. No one knew how to help me prepare. I sensed that they, and Laura, suspicioned that all of this might be a little too good to come true.

"I know you're God's gift to farming, but I sure hope you know what you're doing here," Laura said.

I brought the letter to Mr. Martin and the guidance counselor. "What do I do at the interview?"

They told me that I would be asked about my grades and how hard I studied. I would be asked about my hobbies and what sports I played.

When I asked what I should tell them, the guidance counselor raised both his hands, shrugged and said, "Just be honest."

They were wrong about the interview. I drove to 100 Milk Street again, but this time I was shown to a neatly furnished office on the second floor. A flag stood clamped upright in a corner and a picture of President Eisenhower hung on the wall facing me. The officer who interviewed me, Lieutenant Commander Ryan, sat erect, dressed in a gold-trimmed, blue uniform and crisp, white shirt. All but a few of his questions dug into what I planned to study if won the scholarship. I fumbled them badly. I had only a vague idea of what people studied in college. I knew that people studied agriculture, so I gave that as one answer. He asked me how I did in math. I told him I did OK, but I didn't like math all that much. He did ask me if I worked after school, and I told him about the farm. He told me I would hear from him in a week or so. He stood and provided me with a solid handshake and a polite good-bye, but I knew I didn't do well.

During the wait to hear the results of my interview, I discovered that the navy automatically sent the names of applicants, like me, who did well on their written tests to colleges with NROTC programs. Notre Dame and Boston College sent me letters telling me that if I was accepted by the navy, I could consider myself accepted by them. I should have been excited. Notre Dame and Boston College were favorites among people in Framingham. But I knew for sure I had messed up my interview.

The letter from Lieutenant Commander Ryan started off with good words about my record and my appearance, but then veered to my rejection. He said my obvious career path should be farming and agriculture. Those were not the skills a navy pilot needed. He wrote that the navy needed to use their scholarships for men to study engineering and similar courses.

I felt I had missed my only chance at the brass ring on the merry-go-round. As I suspected, my family had thought the whole time that it was a long shot. Laura saw it differently. She was always on her guard about being tricked, about someone putting something over on her. She became angry that I had been given bad advice. As she often did, she proclaimed suspicions about "stuff going on that we never know about." She insisted that I should "write to the goddamned navy and tell them what happened."

I told her I didn't think that would do any good and that I wasn't ready for college, anyway. The thought of four more years of school put me off. Besides, I teased, Notre Dame was an all-boys school.

. . . .

Grace Krill kept slogging along on the contract. She reworked one detail after another, and always toward her own favor, it appeared to us.

None of us spoke much, but I could tell that each one was wondering how hard it was for the others. The Parks and Earlys on our neighbor farms had already gone through much of the same and were sad for us, but they had spent most all their sadness already.

Over the winter we called people we knew, other farmers and dairymen, to come and take a look at what we had coming for sale at the auction. Those who came said that what we had looked good, and some said they would be back. We sold all our heifers to a man in Stockbridge, which gave us some cash and let us shut down the small barn. A man wanted our pickup, but it was proving a hard winter, and we needed it to plow.

All things considered, we stayed content, enjoyed our holidays, and, I guess, walled off thoughts of what lay ahead. Piece by piece, we glimpsed how it would go. The Boss and Pop would surely go to Maine; Uncle Carl would take one of the offers he always had; and my mother would stay with her job and get absorbed back into her family downtown. My father's business in Worcester now readily supported him and his new family. Each one said I should come with them, but I knew I couldn't, and I think they knew it, too.

I saw them all going their ways without me.

....

The dam cracked in March when Grace Krill came by. The Boss took her to sit at the big oak desk where she spread out a map. I stood aside.

"My surveyors have been over this, and we can't get as many lots on the property as we thought. The hill is too steep here, and we can't get a road in on that side," Grace pointed.

The Boss spun the map around and studied it.

"We may have to look at the price again," Grace said.

The Boss slowly rolled up the map and handed to Grace. "We'll not be taking any less."

Grace nodded and shook her head a bit and left.

"It was just a bargaining trick," the Boss said to me.

I wasn't sure sending Grace away like that was a good idea. I thought about what would happen in only a few weeks with the auction set.

Mr. Gordon, our lawyer, came out to talk with us. He had us sit at the kitchen table and explained that, "It's what they do. I know the Krills, and by now, they have drawings with all the roads laid out and plans for every lot right down to the water. Grace may already be counting her money."

I felt uneasy about Grace Krill's words. I saw how we could be backed into a corner where we couldn't farm and would have to sell for so little that we wouldn't even be able to pay off the bank.

"What about truck farming?" I asked. "George Swenson told me his family plans to go over to all vegetables; no cows, no dairy, just grow vegetables and sell them in Boston. They don't have that much more land than we do."

The silence around the table let me know that my idea owned no ready market. Pop was seventy and worn down; my father had made his break; and Uncle Carl had already acknowledged a different future. It was Mr. Gordon and the Boss who spoke to the reality that I feared.

"I have no feel for that kind of a business for Hillcrest Farm," Mr. Gordon said. "But if you are truly worried, you might want to look into it."

"All I can tell you is that we won't give away our farm to Grace Krill and her family," the Boss said.

In April, the dam broke wide open. I came out of the dairy to see Mr. Gordon pulling his black Cadillac into our yard. He held out a newspaper.

"I thought you and your family might like a copy of today's *Globe*." His smile spread the whole way across his wide face. He called out that we should telephone him after supper. He drove off before I could ask him anything.

The Boss spotted a circle around a small story on an inside page. The story told about a scheduled meeting where Governor Paul Dever was going to reveal his new transportation plans.

That night, Mr. Gordon sounded excited when he talked to us. The Boss held the phone so that Pop, Uncle Carl, and I could hear.

"I've been on the telephone with some friends in Boston. The governor is going to make a big announcement about the Massachusetts Turnpike."

"What does that mean to us?" the Boss asked.

"Well, the governor has finally wrangled the OK for eminent domain out of the legislature, so the Mass Pike is going forward. My friend nabbed a look at the plans, and they showed the Pike passing right through Hillcrest Farm. It means you're sitting on top of an important intersection of the Mass Pike and Route 9. It also means you won't be growing any vegetables and Grace Krill won't be building any houses on your place."

The uproar over the turnpike filled television reports and the newspapers with speculation over what it meant. Who would make money?

What would happen to real estate prices? Who would build it? What would happen to people and businesses in the way of the Pike?

The stories made it seem we now owned a prime piece of property. It took Grace Krill two days before she came to see us. She had no smile for me this time. She joined Pop and the Boss at the kitchen table. Again, I stood aside.

"I want you to know that my family and I will do a first-rate job of commercial and industrial development on Hillcrest Farm," Grace said in a strong level voice. "We might look at raising the price a bit, but I think you'll agree, we do have a deal in place."

"We have no 'deal' in place or anyplace," the Boss said with her down Maine voice. We'll be talking with Mr. Meyer Gordon, our lawyer."

"If you reject the deal we have on the table, there might be some legal trouble," Grace said, frowning.

"Mr. Gordon advised us that might be your position."

In an awkward silence, Grace stood and left us in the kitchen.

"Does that mean she is going to sue us?" I asked.

The Boss seemed unconcerned. "Mr. Gordon says that whenever the Krills don't get their way, they sue."

In the days during the uproar about the 'pike, Walter Brewer and some of the other farmers called to find out what we were going to do. They were pleased for us, and that made us feel good. Laura baked a cake with white frosting and put the 4H Club clover on it with dollar signs in green frosting.

Mr. Rawlings became one of the last ones to let go of his little farm. Laura's mother had passed away, and he and Laura moved to a stone cottage beyond the dam. In May, Laura and I fished there when a hatch of small, blue wing olive flies floated like dark dots over orange and gold reflections. Everyone on the farm had stopped teasing me about Laura, and no one at school paid much attention to farm kids spending time together. We took a break from fishing and looked for some good stones for Laura to paint. I found one that was round and shiny, almost like a silver dollar. We flopped onto the bank.

"What's going to happen?" she asked the river. We told each other the only things we knew for sure—that all that we grew up with was fading away, and we were facing empty space. Neither one of us had any plot to our lives. The war had changed everything.

We sat in silence until she volunteered, "I suppose I'll need to stay and look after my father. Dr. Winter said he would train me to be his dental assistant if I wanted."

I nodded. She pulled her knees up to her chest, tilted her head, and frowned at me, waiting to hear my thoughts. But I had no thoughts or prospects beyond the spring and the end of Hillcrest Farm.

....

My family imagined so many things that could happen now; how we would all have money and do what we wanted in our private dreams. Because I always worried about how little I knew, I kept my dreams make-shift and easy to shake off.

We still had a farm to run and worked hard to put chunks of time together to meet with engineers and surveyors. It surprised me how fast these people worked. In less than two weeks, we met at Mr. Gordon's office where we all sat around a huge table made of wood that glowed reddish gold.

Mr. Gordon spread out a large map of the farm and prepared to describe his ideas. He began by telling us that commercial development was not like building houses. It could take years to develop Hillcrest Farm into a full industrial park.

"Those are years of risk that tie up money," he said, "which means nobody gets a big check up front. But we can do better than the Krills's offer."

He knew what we owed the bank, and he knew that the Krills's offer, plus the money from the auction, would barely cover our debt, leaving us almost nothing.

Then he started smiling and looking at each one of us in turn. As his smile spread, he told us that in addition to our farmland, we had some-thing almost as good as a gold mine. We had our own hill, left by a glacier, and it held tons of clean gravel. He said he had never seen a better spot for such a hill. The state intended to bridge the river and build an inter-section with Route 9 right in front of our hill, and they needed gravel. Mr. Gordon said some men had formed a company and were very inter-ested in buying Hillcrest Farm and our hill, which they now liked to call "The Mountain." He said the developers, Michael Campanelli and Mar-tin Cerel, and the contractor, Lou Perini, who owned the Boston Braves, were some of the partners in the company.

I imagined a huge windfall, with money to fix everything. But then Mr. Gordon described their offer and terms. They would take over both the bank debt and the deed to the farm. The auction money was ours to keep. Mr. Gordon pressed his hands palms down on the table and waited for the offer to sink in.

"Nothing is going to be dug out of the hill for some time, and construction will be spread out for years. That means that the buyers will put up a good down payment right away, but most of the money would be spread over several years. The money is guaranteed, and it will be enough to take fine care of Enoch and Myrtle forever," Mr. Gordon said to Uncle Carl and me.

His words swept away my flimsy dreams of quick wealth and left me with my very short list of choices. It was too late for college and anyway, I didn't want to go. I knew I wouldn't do well cooped up for four years. All I knew was the farm. There was nowhere to farm, and I hated the thought of a factory.

. . . .

It was common enough for boys like me to go into the service. "It makes a man of them," they said. For me, it had to be the navy. I met with the navy recruiter on the second floor of the post office building downtown next to the Farmers and Mechanics' Bank. A brass sign on his desk read C. Scott, Chief Petty Officer, US Navy. After shaking my hand and almost before I sat down, he asked, "Why do you want to join the navy?"

"My father and my uncles were in the navy. I want to be a pilot," I said. "But I don't have any college."

"That doesn't have to be a problem," he said and reached into his desk for a pad of paper. He asked about my father, what he did and where he had been stationed. He asked more questions about me and my family. He wanted to know what kind of work I liked and what I was good at. He wanted to know about my grades and if I was healthy.

I didn't tell Chief Scott about my test and interview for the NROTC program because I didn't want him to think I had already messed up.

Then he pulled a folder out of his desk and said he had a test to see if I could make it into flight training. The test took less than ten minutes.

"You scored right at the top!" he said as he spun around his scoring sheet so I could see it. "Look, you're at the very the top in everything."

He read my skepticism. "Now, this one test doesn't get you into flight training. When you get to boot camp, you tell them about your father and your uncles and how you want to be a pilot. They'll give you another test like this and a special physical, then they send you to Pensacola, Florida where they train pilots. You're not color blind, are you?"

I nodded, "No."

"Then I don't see any problem. You'll be like Mike Wilkie from Sax-onville. He was a farmer, just like you. Enlisted last June and now he's a Cadet, down there in Pensacola learning how to fly."

He gave me the papers to bring home to sign.

After I came out of the post office building, I walked around down-town to look in the stores. Some of the storefronts had become empty, and some other stores looked shabby. All the shops in the Prindeville Arcade were closed. Gilchrest's department store windows were so cloudy I could hardly see what they were selling. The aluminum window frames showed pitting. Very few people were walking around. The newspaper said the downtown stores were still losing business to Shopper's World and the other stores on Route 9. The traffic jams at the rail crossing that ran through the middle of town and the lack of parking got blamed, but it seemed to me that downtown was just old, and I could see no way that it could be fixed back to the way it was before the war.

. . . .

In late May, we all got to-gether and bought Pop a new dark-blue Pontiac Chieftain. Soon after, he and the Boss drove down to Camden, Maine and found a white house with a flower garden and a picture win-dow looking out on a broad lawn that sloped to the sea. They made a deposit before they drove home.

The *Framingham News* printed a picture of Pop, Uncle Carl, Mr. Gor-don, and all the people who bought the farm, signing the papers. Mr. Campanelli and Mr. Cerel were in the picture, but Mr. Perini wasn't.

. . . .

Our high school graduation was a simple affair but one that lasted long enough to make us wonder if we would ever enter the real world. All thoughts were on the graduation parties going on that night at half a dozen kids' houses around town. Keeping to ourselves, Laura and I floated from one to another. The mood at some parties was joyous and rowdy, while at some we sensed an atmosphere of probing and uncertainty. For some partygoers, this was just a small stop-off. They would go from Framingham High into a job at GM or into some office downtown or a college classroom.

Neither Laura nor I drank, and we began to feel out of place in the wet chumminess of the evening's progress. A quiet filled the truck on the drive back to her place. We knew this was an end time for us. When we parked, I asked her if she was sad or angry.

"No," she said. "I just don't know what's going to happen now. This is so different. I don't know what I'm supposed to do."

I turned her toward me and said, "Remember the first time we went swimming off the trestle? We stood out there, and I told you to just close your eyes and jump. You did fine."

"But we were holding hands the first time we jumped," she said. Before I could come up with a good thing to say, she slowly opened the door and stepped out. She looked at me for a second or two, shut the door, and walked to her front gate. I started the truck and shut down my mind.

....

With decisions made and school ended, a calm settled over us like a dome. My perception sharpened. Every object, action, and sound stood out. I felt how the wood shavings slid out of my hand as I spread them and heard the soft puff when they landed. The smell of warm milk, when I poured it over gauze into a stainless can, turned the little milk room into the center of the universe. I watched Pop tease the calico barn cats and waited for his chuckle. On those last few mornings, he walked with me and the cows down to open the pasture gate. I went by the tractor with the battery box I had jumped from when Uncle Carl saved me, but my legs were now much too long for me to think about sitting on it.

The stalls for Tom and Jerry had long ago been stuffed with machinery parts, left over rolls of tar paper, and odd cans that had needed to be got-

ten out of the way. A part bag of cement sat next to a pile of sand for a job I'd never get to now. Only a week or so had gone by since we stopped working, but already I could see dust and faint cobwebs forming everywhere.

I left Pop at the grain room, took my fishing rod from the pegs, and walked down to the river.

I found a good early hatch of flies. They were Hendricksons, but my father used to call them red quills for the way he tied his artificials. I waded and fished from the top of our stretch to the bottom and realized that, except for Laura, I had never seen anybody else fish this water.

. . . .

The day before the big day, a dozen people called "stagers" came to organize the auction. Houghton's company man did come ahead and bought the milk trucks out before they were offered. A dairyman from Shrewsbury put in a telephone bid for the customer lists. We were glad that one of the Scoulos family from the Wellworth downtown picked out most of the equipment from the ice cream stand.

Pop and the Boss knew they couldn't bear watching the auction, so the night before, Uncle Carl and I took them to dinner at the Abner Wheeler House where we all acted as though tomorrow would be just another day of chores and milking and mowing and putting up milk in the dairy. The Boss showed us pictures from Maine, of their white two-story house with dark-blue shutters, a flower garden alongside, and the ocean in the background.

Uncle Carl used the evening to tell us he had taken the job with the tractor dealer in Meredith, New Hampshire, and that Rita and their kids were already packed and ready to go. He decided, with all the changes going, he might as well buy his first new car, a two-tone Dodge Royal.

In the farmyard the next morning, as the Boss and Pop set off for Maine, we hugged, and through sad smiles, told each other to be careful and to be sure and write and how we'd see each other soon.

Uncle Carl and I stood at the top of the drive and watched the shiny blue Pontiac pull out onto Route 9 and head off to Maine. He put his hand on my shoulder and left it there until they went out of sight.

"Time to do it," he said and started walking toward the auction platform.

. . . .

Gus Tanner, the strapping auction manager, acted all business—suit coat off and tie loosened. His size and huge voice overwhelmed the two of us as we reintroduced ourselves. He went over the rules again and asked if we had any questions or if we had anything else we wanted to pull. Uncle Carl shook his head no. By ten o'clock, the farmyard filled up with cars

and trucks, and one of the stagers was obliging people to park in the poison ivy field I had burned clear with Pop. Everyone attending the auction had to file through a makeshift gate to register and get a special yellow card with a bidding number.

Gus told Uncle Carl and me to walk around, pretend we were bidders, and talk up the items people appeared to be pondering. We slid into groups of people who formed up around equipment they wanted to bid on. They elbowed each other to get a better look and to get positioned for when Gus came to call for prices.

After a bid closed, some people would disperse and others would flow into another clutch of bidders for something else. We pretended to be eager to buy. John Le Blanc, who sometimes worked on our tractors, recognized Uncle Carl and came over to say how he could imagine how we all must feel.

"You hung on longer than the rest. This just isn't a place for dairy farms anymore. Carl, you and yours have a new season of life," he said, and reached to shake Uncle Carl's hand.

A special auctioneer worked the big crowd of bidders for the cows. He set it up so that he would call for bids on all the livestock as a parcel, and whoever won the bid could bargain on his own with people who wanted one or two animals in particular.

My father stopped by at lunchtime and brought Uncle Carl and me sandwiches. He drove up in his new truck with Peterson Dairy painted on the side. He walked around for a while, looking for anything he might want to take. He settled on some old milk bottles from the days when bottles were round and had a baby's face molded into the top section. A sketch of the farm was etched in brown beneath the name Hillcrest Farm in old English letters. Our phone number ran around the base of the bottle.

He talked with Uncle Carl for a while, and then came and said he and I should take a walk. We walked around the crowds and out to the concrete platform behind the dairy where Charlie used to drop his hubcaps. As always, he looked me straight in the eye when he talked to me.

"Do you need a ride to the Navy Center tomorrow?" he asked.

I told him I had a ride. I knew if he drove me, he would have to miss a day's deliveries, and that would be hard to make up by himself. He seemed relieved but sad.

"You're smart and tough. You'll do fine in the navy."

He walked close up to me, grabbed me in a hug, turned me loose and then reached out and ruffled my hair. I took it as a signal to walk back up into the auction yard. He waved once to Uncle Carl, got in his truck, and drove off.

....

Midafternoon, I felt a tap on my shoulder and turned around into a waiting hug from Laura. "I couldn't miss this," she said.

She was just in time to see Gypsy auctioned off separately. She had wanted the big mare, but had no place for her. We watched a smaller cluster of women, some with men I took to be vets or farriers, maneuver around Gypsy to get a look at her from every angle. We whispered to each other, wondering if the auctioneer had told them about Gypsy's ears or her fear of bridges.

Around three o'clock, the noise level of the crowd suddenly swelled. The item up for sale was the milk wagon Uncle Carl built when the war started. We had kept it shedded so, with its red, white, and blue paint still glossy, it looked like it had just been built. After a long bidding war, Gus sold it for $900 to the man who ran the Big "E" fairgrounds.

Around three o'clock, Uncle Carl called me aside.

"I'm going to leave," he said. He kept looking away from me, running his hand through his hair. "We can make Meredith before dark. Get settled in."

"Yeah," I said.

"You can handle this OK? Gus will make up the list of what sold and for how much, show you his cut, and tell you how much he'll send to Meyer Gordon's office. That's it."

I nodded yes.

He said I should come up and see him as soon as I could. He told me Meredith is nice and has good fishing, too. By now he was tearing and turned away trying to hide it.

"Douglas, I never thought in my life this could happen. I planned spending my whole life right here. John Le Blanc is wrong. This isn't a new season for us. Seasons repeat and come again. For us, there is no repeat."

We stood silent for some time, looking away toward the water. "Go," I said. He put his hand to my cheek like he did when I was little.

"By the way, what did you think *sot pjoike* meant?"

"I thought it meant 'sweet boy' or 'nice boy,' something like that."

"Nah. It means dumb ass."

We laughed and hugged one last time, and Uncle Carl walked to his new car where Rita and his kids were waiting. I waved and they were gone.

I was glad Laura came to the auction. She stood with her shoulder pressed into me as one part of my life after another got paid for and taken away from me by strangers. Near the end of the bidding, she pulled away and said it was time to say good-bye. We walked to her pickup and leaned against it, holding hands. She blushed and gave me the shiny stone I had found at the river, painted with Douglas on one side and Laura on the other.

"Will you write to me when I'm in boot camp?" I teased. She threw me her narrow-eyed look.

"Of course. And you are going to write to me. And then you're going to come home for a few days and then go off somewhere far away; somewhere I can't go."

"But I'll be coming back."

"That's not so. You're not coming back, not really, not ever. Maybe visits, but not really."

"Maybe you can come with me."

I turned her to me and kissed her a long, soft kiss. I felt her full strength pull me to her and then quickly release me. "I'm not going anywhere."

We both understood what she meant. She took both my hands and squeezed and shook them and I saw the tears. She let go and walked toward her truck. "I'm going to miss you," she called out over her shoulder. It sounded strong and plain and fierce. It sounded like Laura.

. . . .

I stayed with my mother and brother the night before I left for the navy. She had put together a good-bye party. That afternoon, she asked me to sit with her in the kitchen while she made ravioli and simmered her sauce.

"I'm sorry about how everything has worked out," she sighed. "When the war ended, it looked like blue skies forever, but it didn't turn out that way. I don't know what happened."

She stopped still and looked around the kitchen, lost for a minute in her incomprehension. I started to say something, but she brightened and turned back to me.

"I bet you'll like the navy," she said with a real smile. I smiled back and said I was sure I would.

That night, my cousins brought pizza from Bonoldi's bar. We rowdied around her kitchen table drinking beer and playing our own special version of Briscola, an Italian card game where a player took tricks by having the higher card. We were skilled at slipping high cards back out of our discards and using them again. Partners slickly pretended to be confused and would reach across to pull and play cards from each other's hands to the cries of melodramatic outrage from the other players. Wives would look over players' shoulders and clumsily signal what they saw to their husbands. Moans and groans rose with each deception and turn of a card. My brother Ken, only eleven now, used the warmhearted disorder to steal sips of beer and showed a definite wobble as the night went on. I caught my mother watching me every minute.

I had sold the Jeep to my cousin John. He offered to drive me into the Navy Center in Boston, but I asked him to drive me up to the farm instead. I wanted one last look around, and then I could hop the Boston-bound B & W bus in front of Don Crawford's ESSO station.

John dropped me off at the foot of the drive, next to the old black-and-white Hillcrest Farm sign. We shook hands, and he held on to mine for a second.

"This is tough, I know," he said. I thanked him and watched him drive away in the Jeep.

I stopped at the foot of the driveway, as though holding still could keep this from happening. I couldn't go back because it wasn't there, and I didn't want to go forward because that was toward the end.

With each step across the yard, my boots made a two-note crunch that echoed back from the cement wall of the empty dairy. I drifted back and forth across the yard, stunned by the sensation of silence where there had always been ceaseless sounds of life: rattling glass in the dairy, grumbling tractors and trucks, humming pumps and generators, baying animals,

Pop hammering, the Boss calling out. A gritty breeze carried none of the smells I had known all my life: animal smells; sawdust; chlorine from the dairy; and *ny jord*, new earth. The breeze cartwheeled someone's yellow bidding ticket across the yard where it lodged, upright, against the milk house step.

All the doors –the house, the sheds, the dairy, even the big barn doors – had been left open. I imagined the stagers scuttling around at the end of the auction to be sure nothing remained that they could sell or scavenge. The emptiness befit the silence. But I wasn't alone: I caught the flit of a calico barn cat, probably looking for Pop and the warm milk spray.

A steam shovel with a claw-bucket sat poised beside the silo, ready, I imagined, to reach up and claw the big cupola off the top of the barn. Pop told me it was a lantern cupola, built tall with lots of glass to fetch light into the now bare hayloft.

I stood on the Boss' habitual mark in the center of the yard. From there I could see everything: the lower meadow and the pastures, empty of cows, the fields no one would mow again, the secluded river this farm boy had fished for the last time. It all still appeared as timeless as I thought it would be, but now it was vanishing and I had no place to come home. I felt the whole world hold its breath for just a minute. Then it was done.

On my walk down the drive to the state road, I turned for one last look. I would have to call Laura about the barn cat.

Addendum

VOICES FROM THE HOME FRONT WW II

Thirty-Eight Remembrances

In their own words

. . . .

VOICES FROM THE HOME FRONT WW II

In their own words

The Contributing Voices

. . . .

World War II affected my world even before Pearl Harbor	Diane Lewis Hanger b. 1933
Joy on the Home Front	Eileen Culver b. 1935
A Girl from NJ Remembers the War Years	Lynne Coppoletta b. 1940

Nine Postings by Robert "Lash" La Rue
Growing Up in a Changing Home Front
Blackout Drills - A Boy's Home Front Memories
Japanese Internment - A Child's Voice from the Home Front
My Home Front in Flux
Chico California, our New Home Front
Starting Over on the Home Front
War's End on The Home Front
The Road to Halfway
Settling Down in Pine Valley after World War II

. . . .

From My Home Front in the Bronx	Eugene Rinaldi b. 1939
Twins Winning the War on the Home Front	Ron Knott b. 1937
We Malin Twins Did Our Part, Too!	Bob and Dick Malin b. 1937
Making Rationing Work	Lyla K. b. 1936
Some Fun on the Home Front	George Terranova, MD b. 1943
Carolina Home Front	Don Parker b. 1934
The Villain in Our Childhood	C. D. Peterson b. 1937
A Boy's Home Front - from Miami	H. C. 'Nick' Nickerson b. 1935
Time Flys	Stephen B. Miller b. 1934
The Wyoming Home Front	Anonymous b. 1937
A Boy's Home Front - 1940's Oglesby, Illinois	James Duncan b.1941
A War Time Memory	Donald Rogers b. 1935
A Boy's Chicago Home Front	Jim Kelly b. 1935
The Post war home front changes	Dr. Donald Gardner b. 1945
The Civil Air Patrol on the Home Front	Bob Mosely b. 1924

(Brother of Zack Mosely, creator of the popular comic strip "Smilin' Jack")

A young life gets direction	Dave Pace b. 1934
Viewing an Eclipse	Anonymous b. 1937
Then and now	Lucia O'Hara b. 1946

Three excerpts from <u>We Were Not Spoiled</u> *by Lucille Ledoux as told to Denis Ledoux.*

In September 2017, fifteen wonderful seniors agreed to sit and share their memories of the war years on the home front. We met at the Elmwood Hall / Danbury Senior Center in Danbury, Connecticut. The Director who brought us together is Susan M. Tomanio, LCSW…

. . . .

To have your story included in my blog please go to
www.homefrontstories.com

Addendum

VOICES FROM THE HOME FRONT WW II

In their own words

....

World War II affected my world even before Pearl Harbor
Diane Lewis Hanger b. 1933

Many young men of Carmel, as was true across the U.S., joined the military before the outbreak of the war, realizing the country's involvement was inevitable. My brother Carlyle, 18 years my senior, enlisted in the U.S. Army Air Corps in January, 1941. My 7-year-old mind, then, was focused on his activities as he progressed through advanced photographic school at Lowry Field in Colorado to become a Staff Sergeant and gunner/photographer. Pearl Harbor brought us into the war, and I was proud of Carlyle and confident our country would prevail.

I listened intently to nightly news, tracing the war in Europe and the Pacific, read newspapers to follow our troops' movements and kept a list of the dozens of war correspondents. The progress of the war was a constant conversation in our home. In my young mind, there was no possibility we would lose the war.

I earned a nickel every time I brought a letter from my brother from the post office. And I was encouraged to write to all my uncles and cousins who were in the service via V-mail (Victory-mail). I wrote each letter on a special stationery sheet, which folded to form its own envelope. These letters, then, were censored, put on film, and sent to their overseas destination, a method that conserved space in transporting them, then printed again to deliver. I learned that servicemen didn't want serious news, and filled my letters with details of everyday events in the family's life and happenings in Carmel.

Family members served on both fronts. I lost a cousin on Omaha Beach, another, a paratrooper, was wounded shortly after. One lost his life at Pearl Harbor. My uncle, the oldest in the family to serve, fought to capture South Pacific islands from the Japanese. The youngest cousin to serve was a Seabee, building airfields on those islands as we won them. A lot of emotion for a youngster, but I remember feeling immensely proud, and confident we were doing what we had to do to secure peace.

Support for our servicemen was everyone's responsibility. Young men hitchhiked for rides from Fort Ord when they had a weekend pass, and we were always delighted to help them on their way. We invited them into our home for meals sometimes. I remember feeling proud that there was something we could to do to help.

Carlyle's 4th Mapping Squadron fought in the Battle of the Coral Sea, but just prior to shipping out, he was pulled out and chosen to go to South America, instead, with a select group of photographers who had been trained in a new, intricate aerial mapping procedure, with the task of replacing maps which had been produced by Germany and were, therefore, unreliable. Their work was highly successful, and during the months he was there, avid outdoors man that he was, he fulfilled the dream of fishing and hunting in an exotic land of crocodiles and jaguars and tropical fish.

Ironically, my Dad had been instrumental in erecting a large boulder monument in Devendorf Park in Carmel to honor the hometown servicemen who would be the casualties of war. At that time there was just one name, Gordon Bain, brother of my friend Linda, who had joined the R.A.F. and died in England in 1942. This monument was dedicated on Memorial Day, 1942. On the following day, my family learned that my brother, Carlyle's name would be the second name on that stone. As his group returned to the U.S., their plane crashed in a storm in the jungle near Bogatá, Colombia. No one survived. He was 28 years old. My parents grew old that day, and I grew up.

We devoted an area of our garden to a Memory Garden for Carlyle. Fishponds, oak trees, ferns and flowers, and thoughtful additions from family and friends. My father erected a flagpole and raised the flag that had flown over Carlyle's military grave in the Canal Zone every morning. My sister Doris and I lowered it each evening and folded it respectfully. My father was too old to join the service, but that's what he wanted to do. Instead, he gave up his career as a builder for the duration of the war and worked at the Presidio of Monterey as foreman of the carpentry shop, finding himself in charge of German prisoners who were there. I think it helped him cope.

There are twenty names on the memorial plaque in the park in Carmel. I had occasion to write their stories in a book, "Carmel's Heroes," in 2009. http://www.pineconearchive.com/carmelsheroes.pdf.

It was an honor to tell what I could discover about their lives and their bravery, to put faces on those very real people who sacrificed for their country.

Diane Lewis Hanger, 1951

. . . .

Joy on the Home Front

We Won!

Eileen Culver b. 1935

The one thing I remember most is that we all felt like we won out over awful enemies. We were on the good side we all knew. We had worked together as a country. Everyone was very patriotic. You could see flags everywhere. We had shared terrible times but now we were going to be OK.

I felt very proud and happy. Today, I remind myself of those days and wish we still had those feelings.

. . . .

A Girl from NJ Remembers the War Years

How can I remember so much?

Lynne Coppoletta b. 1940

I was born in 1940 in Newark and then moved to Union, where the memories of the war click in.

Lynne, mother Helen, brother Eugene

The dark green light blocking shades.
Daddy's head lights half blocked.
The running board and rumble seat.
The excitement in the streets on VE and VJ day.
Mixing the 'butter' at my neighbor's house. (Don't know what we used)
Saving the 'tinfoil' from gum wrappers.
Party lines at Unionville 2 5057 J
Mom giving me twenty five cents to walk to the store (Heavens, she'd be in jail today) for a few slices of bologna.
Johnny ride a pony - hide and seek - kick the can - sleigh riding on the street in winter - freedom to roam all over the neighborhood.
My first portable radio - looked like a big lunch box.
Climbing and falling out of many trees…..guess I was a real tomboy.

Oh, and I do remember going to the old, old, Newark airport to mail packages to my Uncle Joe who was a cook (chef) in the Navy in the Pacific. (I still have his hat from 1939.) I remember all the things he brought home….a piece of a Japanese Zero, a hand grenade, a bloody Japanese flag.

Lynne at 2 1/2 years old. Wow, as I said, I was born in 1940. It's now 2017. That's a lot of years.

. . . .

NINE POSTINGS BY ROBERT "LASH" LA RUE

Growing Up in a Changing Home Front

Free Verse by Robert LaRue, born 1937

When I was young, about age three,
I sat on a limb, in Grandmother's tree,
And picked avocados,
And ate them.
Nobody told me, I shouldn't like them.
I stood by a fence, when I was four,
Watching truck farmers, on the other side,
Hoe the field,
And pick vegetables.
The children there, wouldn't come play.
Some uniformed men, came to the field,
And talked to the farmers, and took them away,
Leaving the plants,
To wither and rot.
I heard adults say, the Japs are gone.
As a boy growing up, I learned about war,

How our boys overseas, killed Germans and Japs,
To save the world,
For Mother and me.
I learned new words, like Kraut and Nip.

When my turn came, I went down South,
I learned to fly airplanes, and shoot and bomb,
To protect the world,
From Ruskies and Chinks.
Japanese and Germans, were now my friends.

A lad from the west, I found the south odd,
For all public places, contained three Johns,
One said MEN,
One said WOMEN.
One said COLORED, no gender inscribed.

Years passed on by, worlds seemed to collide,
Whites against Blacks, the Vietnam War,
Assassinations,
Demonstrations.
Everyone had a cause, and someone to follow.

Commies and Rednecks, Beatniks and Hippies,
Niggers and Jews, Wetbacks and Gooks,
The Klu Klux Klan,
Watergate.
Everyone had a label, and hated the other.

From college to high-tech, sport cars and aerobics,
Yoga and free love, hallucination,
I tried many fruits,
In search of knowledge.
None seemed to taste, of ultimate truth.

Now my world like that limb, in Grandmother's tree,
Lets me watch from afar, and listen to me,
I eat avocados
Because I like them.
Sometimes, they give me heartburn.

....

Blackout Drills - A Boy's Home Front Memories

Blackout Drills (and my Flashlight)

Robert LaRue, b. 1937.

December 7, 1941 may have been "a date which will live in infamy" for President Roosevelt, but it was the beginning of all kinds of strange and scary events for a four-year-old. The wailing sirens and darkness of blackout drills stand out in my mind.

We lived on a dairy in Baldwin Park, California. Baldwin Park is located only 20 miles from downtown Los Angeles. In the days before supermarkets, it was not uncommon for dairies to be located near population centers. On site retail marketing was a common practice. After the attack on Pearl Harbor, what had been considered a good location for dairy product retailing also came to be considered a prime target for a Japanese attack.

Before radar bomb sights, bombardiers relied on what they could see on the ground to figure out where to release their devastation. A primary means of civil defense against night attack was the blackout drills. If there was no light on the ground, the attackers could not identify their targets. The sound of blackout sirens in the night became a fact of life for us. Rationing also became a fact of life. Living on a dairy, we had plenty of milk to drink, but meat was rationed even for us. To supplement our diet, Dad built some hutches and raised rabbits. He shared the fryers with the dairy's owners, a Dutch family named Cohn, in exchange for alfalfa and grain. Mrs. Cohn also helped with caring for the animals.

One dark night, I was out by the hutches helping Mrs. Cohn when the sirens wailed and the lights went out. She had come prepared for such an event with a flashlight. She handed the flashlight to me to hold while she finished the chores. Like any kid of four, I proceeded to flash the light around and point it at the sky. Sweet, gentle Mrs. Cohn came unglued. She grabbed the offending torch from my little hands and explained to me in no uncertain terms that I could have caused us to be bombed. I suppose she was somewhat oversensitive about bombing since she still had family in Holland who had recently experienced the Blitzkrieg. But she scared the heck out of me. I quickly changed from being a carefree child piercing the night sky with a harmless flashlight to being a magnet for falling explosives.

To this day, I feel a stab of fright any time I allow a flashlight's beam to wander above the horizon at night!

Japanese Internment - A Child's Voice from the Home Front

Japanese Internment from the eyes of a four year old.

Robert LaRue b. 1937

My dad often lets me tag along as he makes his rounds of McMullen Dairy. We live on the dairy in the San Gabriel valley of Southern California. A cacophony of voices fills my memory of these home front times.

Robert "Lash" LaRue c. 1942 with measles required sunglasses

"Elgin, Elgin, come have a wee taste," Mr. McMullen's Scottish brogue rings out from his front porch. We climb the stairs and I watch with the curiosity of a four-year-old as the two men share a glass of wine while discussing the status of the dairy and events of the day. I know my dad's name is Eldon and wonder why Mr. McMullen always calls him Elgin.

"Lash's" dad, Eldon

The house sets back among the trees of McMullen's walnut orchard. I listen curiously to men talking in Spanish as they tend the trees. We take our leave and walk on out to the cow pasture. Dad opens the gate and we follow the cattle down the lane to the holding pen outside the dairy barn. The milkers take over and shout the cries of western herdsmen as they sort and move the milk strings into their respective stanchions.

Pete, the dairy operator, comes out of his house. He scoops me up, swings me around, and teases me in his Dutch accented English. He sets me down and he and my dad discuss the condition of the herd. When the cows are locked in their stanchions, Dad straps on his milking stool, sets his bucket under the first cow of his string, and the never-ending task of a dairy farm begins anew. Pete walks me back to our house and hands me over to my mom.

"Lash's" mom, Dee

Mom is listening to the Hit Parade on the radio. She sends me out to play while she tends to her household chores.

I approach the backyard fence and listen to the singsong voices of the orient coming from the truck farm next door. The people speaking are bent over tending their rows of plants. A pretty little girl about my age leaves the group and crosses the field toward me. She sits down across the fence from me and we play in the dirt.

My parents have tried to explain that these people are Japanese and somehow different. I don't understand. I can see that she is darker than Pete's redheaded granddaughter, Sharon. Her eyes are different. But she is just as fun to play with. We play with few words, but words are not needed. Still, the fence separates us. She does not come to my house and I don't go to hers.

The afternoon wears on. A woman comes and leads the girl away. She smiles and says something that I don't understand. I watch as they walk toward their house. The girl turns and her hand comes up in a small wave. I wave back.

Dad comes home from the afternoon milking. Mom sets out dinner and we eat. After dinner, Dad and I go to the living room while Mom cleans up the kitchen and nurses my baby brother. Dad turns on the radio.

The smooth voice of Lowell Thomas comes over the airways. He tells us the news of the day. Most of what he has to say is about the war. The war is not news to me. Like the endless routine of the dairy, it has always been there. It is a part of our lives. We don't feel it; it is far away. But we hear about it constantly. It is like the sound of the ocean when we camp on Laguna Beach. It rumbles in the background without end.

It is an afternoon like any other. Pete hands me off to Mother. I go out the backdoor to the yard. It is strangely quiet. I can hear the strains of Glen Miller's "Don't Sit Under The Apple Tree" playing from inside the house. But no singsong voices come from the field next door. It is deserted. The plants still stand, green and growing. But no one is taking care of them. The people are gone. I sit by the fence for a while, alone. The death-like silence wraps around me.

I go back in the house and ask my mom where the people have gone. "The Army took them away," she tells me. She tries to explain, but her words are not enough. Not enough to quell the fear welling up inside me. The first chink in my armor of innocence has been opened.

. . . .

My Home Front in Flux

The World Changes

By Robert LaRue b. 1937

As World War II wore on, life on the home front became increasingly chaotic. Everything was in short supply. Ration stamps came into being. The "black market" raised its ugly head. Outside forces were taking over people's lives. Unwelcome regimentation was extending from the military down into the civilian population.

The magician we call memory has many tricks up its sleeve. Trivial things often stand out ahead of major events. Its slight of hand hides some experiences and makes clear others. Perhaps we choose what we remember; perhaps what we remember chooses us.

As a first-born son and grandson, love and security surrounded me. A doting grandmother watched over me while my mom went to business school. Three aunts, age 17, 19, and 21 the year I was born, spoiled me. My world was safe.

I remember bits and pieces. Aunt Sue's idea of babysitting was to strap me in the front seat of a Piper Cub and fly around Southern California as she built up flight hours. She let me take hold of the stick and bank and turn and climb and dive. At least I thought I was in control. I loved it. Aunt Fran had married and her father-in-law lived with them. He had a handcart he pushed around the neighborhood selling fruit and vegetables door to door. I delighted in tagging along as his "helper." Aunt Rae was busy with nursing school but always had time for a hug and a kiss for Bobby.

My memory of the attack on Pearl Harbor and our entry into the war does not stand out. Maybe my parents shielded me from the details. Sometime during those early years, we moved out from the town of Baldwin Park to the foreman's house on McMullan's Dairy. Scary things like the blackout sirens and the disappearance of the Japanese people next door stand out in my memory. Even so, the daily routines of the dairy kept me occupied and maintained my sense of security.

In 1942, kindergarten caught up with me. I reveled in it. My grandfather was Baldwin Park School Superintendent. If I received any celebrity or favoritism from that fact, I was unaware of it. I fell in love with Miss Rice, my teacher. At the end of the school year, our parting was heart wrenching.

Even so, my sense of bliss was not being shared by the world at large. The world was at war. Lives everywhere were in a state of flux. Governments were intruding on people's lives and becoming more and more controlling. My world was about to come apart.

When war broke out, my dad tried to enlist. He was deferred because he worked on a dairy farm and had two children. Three of his siblings did join up. Uncle Len joined the navy and completed Officer Candidate School. Aunt Sue became a Women's Army Service Pilot. Aunt Rae became a Navy Nurse. Dad and Aunt Fran stayed home.

In 1943, an event occurred that is forever blanked from my memory. But it changed my life forever. For reasons that were never made completely clear to me, we were suddenly uprooted and moved from Baldwin Park 500 miles away to Chico, California. It had something to do with the draft board and someone wanting Dad's deferment. Whatever the reason, Dad was transferred from McMullan's Dairy to a dairy on a large farming operation in the Sacramento Valley.

My brother Wes, a neighbor girl, and me on the big farm in Chico

143

The move was traumatic for the whole family. My parents were none too happy. We moved from a cozy bungalow on a showcase dairy to a shack in a row of farm workers quarters. Our new home could have been right out of John Steinbeck's novel, "The Grapes of Wrath." Dad was demoted from Dairy Foreman to common milker. I was torn away from everything I had known for the first six years of my life.

I started first grade in strange surroundings, knowing no one, afraid, and lonely. War on the home front had taken its toll. Miss Rice and my paths would never cross again.

Chico California, our New Home Front

Another war time move

By Robert LaRue b. 1937

As a six-year-old, I do not recall a lot about our move from the row of farm worker's shacks where Dad milked cows into our own place. In my memory, it is as if one day we were there and the next we were at our new home.

Our new 20-acre homestead consisted of a house, a barn, a small nut orchard, and a good-sized plot of fertile Sacramento Valley row-crop land. The orchard consisted of almonds (or as folks around Chico called them, *ammonds*) and walnuts. The cropland lay fallow. The house was much too small to accommodate two families. Grandma and Grandpa and Jimmy needed a home of their own.

For Dad and Grandpa, building a house posed no problem. They were both good craftsmen. The problem arose when they tried to get their hands on framing lumber. Like everything else, lumber was in short supply. The war effort now devoured everything but life's bare necessities. As happened all too often, they were put on a waiting list.

Once more, family came to the rescue. Dad's uncle David and his family lived in Chico. Uncle David worked at a local sawmill. He knew how to cut through enough red tape to get the needed lumber delivered. Dad and Grandpa went to work.

The house went up rather quickly. I don't think it was ever completely finished, but it was finished enough that Grandma reluctantly agreed to move in. At times, you just had to learn to make do on the home front.

In the meantime, Grandpa acquired an old horse and enough implements to start farming. Most folks during the war had small victory gardens. We soon had several acres of victory garden.

Jimmy and I got our initiation into the meaning of hard work from that garden. At Grandpa's direction, we learned to hoe around plants and nurture them into production. Lord help the offender who happened to uproot a watermelon seedling instead of a pigweed. Melons made up the main crop, but there were also, beans, corn, tomatoes, and more. When each crop was ready, we picked and loaded it into Dad's old pickup truck and peddled it to stores around the valley. What we didn't sell, Mom and Grandma canned. We were well fed.

When the nuts were ready in the orchard, we spread tarps on the ground under the trees. We shook the trees by pounding on the trunks with baseball bats padded with pieces of rubber tire. The nuts fell to the ground and we gathered them and put them in sacks. The almonds were easy to shake loose, the walnuts more difficult and required a lot of hand picking on ladders. The whole family participated, even my brother Wes, who was three years my junior.

Dad continued working in the paint shop at the air base. He also continued with the ambulance and accident cleanup crew. In 1944 Chico Air Base switched from basic training to fighter pilot training in P 38 Lightning's. Crashes and deaths doubled from 14 crashes and 8 deaths during the two years of basic training to 35 crashes and 16 deaths during the 16 months of fighter pilot training.

That's more than 2 crashes a month. The ambulance and cleanup crew stayed busy. Dad tried to not show it, but even I could tell that he was under a great deal of stress.

Summers are hot in the Sacramento Valley. Air conditioning was not widely available in the early 1940s. Makeshift evaporation coolers consisted of wet burlap sacks hung from open window frames with fans in front - they were not very effective.

The only real escape from the heat was finding cool water. There was a public swimming pool in Chico, but my parents were afraid of public pools. They believed them to be a likely place to contact the crippling disease polio. So we did not swim there. We did occasionally go down to the Sacramento River to fish, swim, and picnic.

We were enjoying an outing with the Robins family, the family of a friend of Dad's from work, when I decided to take an unsupervised dip. I waded out from shore by myself with confidence. Suddenly the current picked me up and I bobbed down stream like a waterlogged cork. I remember looking up at a bluff, high above the river, and seeing my dad preparing to dive when I felt the welcome arms of Mrs. Robins envelope me. My movements were severely restricted following that incident.

Nineteen forty-three moved on into 1944. My sister Deanne was born in August. The war continued unabated. I started second grade in September. The world at war, farming the land, P 38's from the base buzzing overhead, bickering with Uncle Jimmy, Dad shooting a rabid coyote lurking around our chicken coup, Grandpa trying to start his old car with a hand crank because batteries could not be had and his cussing at it and hitting it with the crank, talk that the war would never end; these things all seemed normal to me. As a seven-year-old, they were all I knew. I had no other frame of reference. As Harry Truman famously said, "the only thing new is the history we don't know."

We of the *last generation* knew no history yet. The canvas remained to be painted.

....

Starting Over on the Home Front

War Disrupts a Family

Robert LaRue b. 1937

Even as a six-year-old, I could sense the change in my parents. I understood my own anxiety. The move from Baldwin Park to Chico had toppled my entire world. But grownups were not supposed to have those feelings. I could only hope that our life would somehow get back to normal.

I did not have long to wait. My dad was a very resourceful man. When the stock market crashed in 1929, he had just turned seventeen. He entered adulthood during very trying times. He was a product of the Great Depression.

His parents were schoolteachers. Thus, education was paramount in their lives. Dad tried to keep peace in the family by remaining in school. But money was short and he was of an independent nature. For the next seven years until he was 24, he alternated between academic pursuits at Northern Arizona State College in Flagstaff and Arizona State College in Tempe, and the "school of hard knocks"; riding the rails and living in hobo jungles throughout the United States. He learned at an early age to be "quick on his feet." Survival required it.

The free life ended in 1936 when he married my mom. They were married on the first of June shortly after Mom graduated from high school. I was born nine months later on March 24. Dad was now a family man.

Dad was up to the task. With the help of my grandparents, he bought a lot in Baldwin Park, California and built a home for us. He went to work for McMullan's Dairy milking cows.

He worked his way up to foreman and we moved into the foreman's quarters on the dairy. My mom helped out in the little store where they sold the dairy products they produced. Despite the war, their life seemed secure.

Therefore, it came as a shock when the government suddenly transferred my dad away from the life they had built. The consequences of war had robbed them of their independence. Their secure life had suddenly evaporated. They were reduced to living in a farm worker's shanty. Dad was back to starting over as a common hand on a large farming operation milking cows. The war had taken control of their lives.

Ever the man of action, Dad set about righting things. Over the next few months, he turned our life back around. He met with the draft board, or whoever controlled such things, and managed a transfer from the dairy to Chico Army Air Field. He bought a twenty-acre farm and moved us into the old house that came with it. *Brother Wes, dad Eldon, mom Dee, sister Deanne* Our new home was far from luxurious, but it was far better than the farm worker's quarters we moved from. My parents were happier. They were regaining control.

The move was like an answer to my prayers. I hated the school I was enrolled in. I felt like I had been dropped into an alien world without a friend in sight. The move came with a change in schools. Whereas the old school had seemed large and impersonal, the new school felt warm and welcoming. It was a rural two-room facility with grades one through four in one room and grades five through eight in the other. The teachers and other students made me feel at home. I could walk to school from our house without taking a bus.

Chico Army Air Field, called "the base" in everyday conversation, was established in 1941 to train pilots. Dad worked in the paint shop. He also rode on or drove the ambulance whenever there was an accident. I can remember him coming home visibly shaken following some of those accidents. He detested that part of his job. But like almost every citizen at the time, he pitched in and did what he had to do to help win the war.

It soon became apparent that being on ambulance call, working full time in the paint shop, and trying to farm all at the same time formed an impossible task. I don't know how it worked, but apparently when you worked for the Army during World War II, you didn't just up and quit because you had something you'd rather be doing. As a consequence, my mom's parents, along with my uncle Jim who was about five years older than me, came out from Arizona to live with us. Grandpa Thompson was a hard rock miner and a farmer. Dad continued to work at the base and Grandpa took over the farm. Sometimes it took family teamwork to survive on the home front.

Eldon LaRue had not forgotten his survival skills. He was still "quick on his feet."

War's End on The Home Front

The end of World War II in 1945 brought many changes to the home front

By Robert LaRue, b. 1937

Germany surrendered in May. In August, the worlds first atomic bombs dropped on Hiroshima and Nagasaki and Japan gave up. Living in the farmlands of the Sacramento Valley, I do not remember a lot about the celebrations that took place. I do remember that shortly thereafter, we were loaded up and on off on a new adventure.

Migration from farm to city marked the American experience from the beginning of the Industrial Age. That movement accelerated during WWII. Although he would not have thought of it in exactly those terms, my dad determined to do the exact opposite. He decided get as far away from city life as he could, own his piece of land, and farm full time. With the war over and the government's control of his movements ended, Dad set about to fulfill his dream.

In short order, he sold our little farm in Chico, California and quit his job at the air base. He loaded our belongings into the back of a 1937 Chevrolet pickup truck, loaded Mom and we three kids into the cab, and headed north. The young hobo of the depression had traded his knapsack in for a truckload of family and possessions. But he was determined to live by his own rules nonetheless.

Dad drove, Mom sat on the right side holding baby sister Deanne, I sat in the middle straddling the gear shift lever, and little brother Wes variously stood and lay down at Mom's feet. Our route over the Sierras remains unknown to me. I do remember stopping at a wayside, perhaps around Lake Almanor, for lunch. A cool breeze wafted through towering Ponderosa Pines, a welcome relief from the summer heat of the Sacramento Valley. The scent of the pines combined with the delicious pan-fried pheasant Aunt Marie had packed in our lunch hamper remain with me to this day.

We pressed on to Alturas, a small ranching center in the northeast corner of California. We arrived in late afternoon. The town was in a festive mood with banners stretched across the main street announcing its annual fair and rodeo. Cowboys and cowgirls, afoot and horseback, lined the streets and sidewalks. We found this all very exciting until we discovered that there was no lodging available. The war was over and it was time to celebrate. People coming out of the hills and valleys surrounding the town had taken every room available.

Lakeview, Oregon is about 55 miles north of Alturas. It was dark by the time we got there. It too was full up with the overflow crowd from its neighbor.

With the aid of a flashlight, Dad found a dot on the map about 85 miles north of Lakeview called Wagontire. We passed through the dark starry night until a small sign and darkened buildings announced our destination. A gas pump, a café, and living quarters for the owners made up the entire town. A lighted window in the living quarters indicated that someone was still awake. Dad knocked on the door with the intention of asking if we could camp in their parking lot.

Perhaps it was learned behavior from his hobo days, or perhaps it was just in his makeup. My dad always exuded an air of quiet confidence and honesty. I like to think it was the latter. Anyway, he explained our plight to the man of the house. The man looked us over, invited us in, and they put us up for the night. Who knows how often the Wagontire proprietors were called upon to tender such an act of charity along that lonely stretch of highway? I can only attest to this one event. And I have no way of knowing if any money changed hands. I am sure that we patronized their café before we departed.

That's just the way things were done out in the country, on the home front, in 1945.

In 1945 a family in Wagontire put us up in their home. Years later the town could boast of a motel.

The Road to Halfway

We leave California and move to the bucolic world of Northeastern Oregon

Robert LaRue, b. 1937

The Wallowa Mountains dominate the landscape of the northeast corner of Oregon. The Nez Perce Indians called this country The Land Of Winding Waters. With the coming of the European settlers, these craggy mountains and picturesque valleys became known as the American Alps. To the east of the mountains the Snake River slices through North America's deepest river gorge, Hells Canyon. Nestled in one of the valleys above the canyon's rim, the little town of Halfway is our destination

Before Halfway however, we make a stop at Nampa, Idaho. An old friend and fellow worker from McMullan's Dairy had established a farming operation there. Dad wants to visit with his friend and check out the area. Our host saddles a horse for me ride. It is my first experience riding a real working saddle horse, and I am hooked. I spend every waking hour riding around the ranch until we leave.

The road leading from Nampa to Halfway follows along the old Oregon Trail to Baker Oregon. Pioneers in covered wagons followed the same route starting in the 1840s. The route runs along the Snake River to a place called Farewell Bend. At Farewell Bend the Snake turns north into Hells Canyon. The Oregon Trail forks off through the Burnt River canyon up to Baker Valley. We pioneers of the 1940s follow this historic route in our 1937 pickup truck.

From Baker we turn east for the next 60 miles to our destination, Pine Valley. We cross the still visible wheel ruts of the Oregon Trail running through a dry sage-covered plain. The landscape changes to a stretch of lush green irrigated pastures and farmed fields. The paved road turns to loose gravel. Passengers in occasional oncoming vehicles wave a friendly greeting as we pass. We seem to travel through time to an earlier era. Cowboys and ranchers still tend their cattle on horseback. Farm implements are still drawn by stout draft horses. The twentieth century has largely eluded the countryside.

Bob "Lash' LaRue bull rider

The road unexpectedly changes back to pavement. The landscape changes to a narrow canyon. We follow the Powder River through deep cuts and winding turns to Eagle Valley. Eagle Valley reveals another landscape of green pastures and farmed fields. We pass through the small cluster of homes and businesses called Richland. The valley closes back to a narrow canyon as we approach the Powder's terminus with the Snake.

A lettered road sign points left to Halfway. We follow the sign and climb a steep grade with sharp switchbacks. Our loaded pickup grinds along in low gear. We top the hill and travel down through a wide swale. Cattle graze on the dry yellow grass below farmsteads set back to a narrow canyon.

We turn left at an intersection near a sawmill and follow the valley's only paved road to Halfway. Halfway boasts a bank, two grocery stores, two bars, several churches, three gas stations, a combined drug and liquor store, and other related businesses. The Gray Gables Hotel houses one of the bars and offers rooms to rent. Three housekeeping cabins behind a white picket fence and a manicured green lawn flank one side of the hotel. We rent one of the cabins and set up housekeeping. It is a welcome relief to get off of the road and out of the confines of the cramped pickup cab.

My eight-year-old mind does not grasp the significance of our travels. At eight, you do not question your parent's actions. You simply accept whatever they do as the norm. Even so, I could sense that this small world was a complete change from the world I had experienced in California. My dad's motivations will always remain a mystery. Perhaps he was a throwback to his grandparent's generation. Perhaps he was a precursor to the counterculture of the 1960s. Maybe he just wanted to escape the controls that a wartime culture had placed on society.

The cold hard facts were that we had arrived in the strangely named little town of Halfway, Oregon and there I would remain for the next ten years until I graduated from high school. My Post-War Home Front had just begun.

Photo Credit: Anna Brisk, Halfway Oregon, and thanks to Cindy and Anna. Bob LaRue, Pine Valley Union High School class of 1955.

Settling Down in Pine Valley after World War II

By Robert LaRue, b. 1937

1884. Following that discovery, the Cornucopia Mines dominated the local economy until 1942 when the War Production Board's Order No. 208 shut down gold mining in the United States.

Without the mines, Cornucopia became a ghost town and Pine Valley's economy became completely dependent upon agriculture and lumbering. When we arrived there in 1945 the valley still contained four towns: Pine Town, Halfway, Jim Town, and Carson. Halfway was the commercial center. Pine Town and Jim Town consisted of a store and gas pump. Carson had no commercial activity. The distance from Pine Town on the south to Carson on the north was seven miles. The valley was three to four miles at its widest. Even so, Pine Valley was still the home of the Baker County Fair. And when the long-time announcer stood in his booth over the bucking chutes each fall and told us that "This is where the pavement ends and the West begins," he spoke straight truth. We definitely lived at the end of the road.

Typical of a rural somewhat closed society, our arrival was regarded with a degree of suspicion by the local residents. Dad was unabashed. His experiences during the depression, on the road, riding the rails, and living hand to mouth had taught him how to assimilate into varying social situations. He quickly found a job as a farmhand. The job came with an old farmhouse near Pine Town. We moved into the house and Mom set up housekeeping. Mom had grown up traipsing around Arizona, following her dad from mining job to mining job. She was no stranger to household moving. When September rolled around I started third grade in my fourth school in as many years.

Pine Town school consisted of two rooms, two outhouses, and a belfry. The extra room may have been utilized in years past, but by 1945 all eight grades were taught in one room by one teacher. Rows of desks bolted down to board rails lined the room. Students were assigned desks with each grade occupying a row or portion thereof. I don't know how she did it, but our country schoolmarm was perfectly capable of maintaining discipline and advancing the three Rs to eight levels of learning without assistance. Perhaps some of today's class size negotiators could use a lesson from Mrs. Krego.

The job Dad hired onto was for an elderly rancher, the descendant of a pioneering family. This gentleman no longer ran cattle but relied on pasture rental and hay sales to support his operation. When the growing season ended, so did the job. However, a neighboring rancher needed a man to feed his herd during the winter, so Dad took that job. We continued to live in the first ranchers house.

Pine Valley has what some call its own mini-climate. Because of the way the prevailing winds create convection currents over the surrounding mountains, the valley receives an inordinate amount of snow. It is not uncommon to find four or five feet of the white stuff piled up on the valley floor during January and February. Cattle are completely dependent on harvested feed and forage for several months each year.

HOME FRONT

When we arrived in 1945, mechanized agriculture was virtually nonexistent. Horse drawn implements were the norm. Ranchers turned their cattle out onto the public grazing lands in the spring. They then spent all summer irrigating their fields and harvesting hay and some small grains for the coming winter.

Some of the hay was hauled in by wagon and stacked loose inside barns. This hay fed the horses, small dairy strings, and family milk cows kept on the farm. The bulk of it was stacked loose in the fields to feed the main herd. The last growth of grass was saved for late fall grazing when the cattle were gathered from the range, sorted by brand, and returned to their home ranches.

When the first snow flew, hay wagon racks were moved onto bobsled runners and the feeding season began. Dad's job was to hitch a team of horses to a bobsled each morning and drive them out to a hay stack. The stacks were fenced off by wood panels. He would open a panel, drive the team and sled alongside the stack, and close the panel. He would then crawl up onto the stack and pitch hay onto the bobsled.

When the sled was loaded, he would crawl down, open the front panel, drive the team onto the field, and close the panel. He would then start the team across the field and pitch hay onto the ground in piles. The cattle would string out behind the sled, feeding from the piles.

As winter progressed and the snow deepened, the feeding area would become a circle. Each day Dad would scatter the hay onto the fresh snow of the circle's perimeter. The cattle would feed off the fresh snow and then bed down on the hay they hadn't eaten. Thus they remained clean and healthy.

The feeding area would expand outward until the haystack was finally exhausted. Moving to the next stack could be challenging. When the snow was deep, Dad would hitch a four horse team to the bobsled. He would load the last hay from the exhausted stack and head the tandem team to the next stack. The lead horses would lunge through the snow breaking a trail while second team would follow along pulling the sled. The cattle would follow the sled, tramping down the snow and creating a path to the new stack. Dad would open the new stack and the process would start all over again with a new circle.

For Eldon LaRue, this was a large departure from the dairy in Baldwin Park, California. Even so, he was again doing something he loved. He had escaped the clutches of the machinery of war. He was once more working with cattle. When thinking of an epitaph following his death, the best I could come up with was: "He was a herdsman by nature and damned good with cattle." RIP to my father who safely guided his family through the challenges of War on the Home Front.

. . . .

From My Home Front in the Bronx

What I Remember

Eugene Rinaldi b. 1939

I was born in November of 1939 and my memories of the war are vague for two reasons: because I was too young and because I'm too old.

My first memory involves listening to reports from the Battle of the Bulge (Dec. 1944 to Jan. 1945) on the floor model Philco (might have been Motorola) radio in our living room in the Bronx. Calling it a living room is a great exaggeration, but it's where we lived.

My father was an air raid warden. When the sirens went off, he would patrol the streets to be sure all the lights were out and the shades were drawn. I remember sitting with him listening to the radio in the dark. I had turned 6 years old in November. I have no idea who the reporter was, but my father and I listened with rapt attention. Today, I have a problem with the difference between what I heard or what my father told me.

He said - or the radio reported - that it was so dark that men in the field were wearing something like a miner's helmet. For years I never thought to question this tactic. But, if you're in a battle, why in God's name would you put a light on your head? Wouldn't that be the best target for an enemy? Anyway, that's my recollection of the radio in 1945, and my earliest memory of the war. (I suppose I should do some research and find out if there is any truth to my memory.)

Of course, there were the daily routines we all remember: rationing, war bonds, paper and metal drives. I remember soaking cigarette papers, the ones with tin foil on one side, to remove the tin foil, We rolled it into balls the size of a baseball. They were collected by 'the junk man' with his horse and cart, to aid the war effort.

And I remember victory gardens. I lived with my parents and three sisters, my grandparents, an aunt and a married uncle and his wife in a three-family house at 4617 Matilda Ave. between 240th and 241st streets in the Bronx. My grandfather, a boot black, bought the house in 1927. The neighborhood was pretty nice, it was called Wakefield.

Our victory garden was four or five flower boxes on the back porch filled with basil, parsley and oregano. But on the corner of Matilda Avenue and 241st St. sat the real thing: an acre of corn, potatoes, cabbages, zucchini and tomatoes. Mr. Spoto, who owned the garden, guarded it like it was Fort Knox.

From Left to Right Joseph A. Matturro b.1938,(Big Joe); Eugene J. Rinaldi b.1939 (Genieboy); Ralph C. Odierna b.1939 (Butch); Joseph P. Matturro b. 940(Little Joe). All my second cousins - our grandmothers were sisters. We were around 6 or 7 yrs. old

None of my seven uncles, from both sides of my family, were in the service, while my second cousins had three uncles in the service. This was a cause of great embarrassment and envy on my part but I managed to bear that burden.

They were Anthony (Uncle Tony) Sgt.US Army; Domenic (Uncle Dick) Captain US Army Air Force and Vincent (Uncle Vinny) 2nd Class P.O.US Coast Guard. They were first generation Italians, and of course heroes to us. We learned from them that famous army song "Gee Ma I wanna Go Home". It took a couple of days for me to figure out that "Geema" was not a geographic war location.

My uncles were second cousins once removed but I was taught to call them uncle out of respect for their age. Three sons, one family, I'm impressed even now. And they were great guys to boot, who never ceased to fascinate us with their war stories.

VJ DAY is my most vivid memory and that's a little clouded. It was August of 1945. There was no school (I would have been in kindergarten that year) and my father took me into the streets of the Bronx with him. It was evening, I had my pajamas and slippers on as we walked Matilda and Carpenter avenues. The pure and overwhelming joy was incredible. I still feel it to this day. People on their stoops, people hanging out their windows, people delirious, banging pots and pans, hollering, shooting off fireworks, laughing, crying, I never witnessed anything like it before. I have no Idea how long we stayed out, but the memories of the guys parading in their cars, people on the fenders, in the rumble seats, and on the running boards, it was just fantastic.

We may never see anything like that night again. But one thing is for sure: Tom Brokaw was right. The men and boys who fought that war were, without a doubt, "The Greatest Generation".

....

Winning the War on the Home Front

How My Twin and I Helped Win the War

Ron Knott b. 1937

EARLY MEMORY
When my twin brother, Roland, nick name Roe, and I were born we lived in the Village of Noble, LA. Noble was a village of about 200 souls in 1937. The town had been much larger around 1900, as several large sawmill companies moved in and logged the thousands of acres of virgin pine timber. They brought in hundreds of Spanish families from Mexico for the hard labor. After the large sawmills cut all the timber and moved on, the Spanish stayed on at Sabine River about 10 miles west of Noble, so there were a lot of Spanish in our school.

NOBLE, LA

During the time of the big mills, Noble was one of the largest cities in Sabine Parish. Noble had a bank, drug store, two big saw mills, and a big commissary. By the time we were born, though, all industry had left Noble and it had only three small grocery stores and a post office. Noble was a sleepy bedroom community. They did have a high school.

OUR HOME

I was told that we lived in the Cox house at the time of my birth. It was a rental place with no central heat or air condition. My dad bought what was the office from the large timber company and that became our home. I saw the check years later that he paid $700 for the building. It was only about 1200 s/f. They were able to make three bedrooms out of this small office. Granny had one bedroom, Aunt Maggie and Onnie, her son, had a bedroom, and Momma, Dad, Roe, and I had the other. I don't remember it being so, but I am sure we were very crowded. They made a kitchen out of a couple of joining closets. No bathroom. We used a wash tub out near the well to take a bath. I still remember that cold water.

Twins Roe and Ron Knott

The house did have a large front porch with two big swings that were good for cooling down in the evening. Also, my mother would swing us and sing Christian songs until we went to sleep at night. I still remember those sweet soothing songs.

NO SEWER/RUNNING WATER

The Village of Noble had no sewer or water system. Our "out-house" was about 150 feet behind the main house and it sure was dark and cold making that necessary journey in the winter time. My grandmother used a 'slop-jar' in her room during the night an emptied it early in the morning.

A 'slop-jar' was a big mouth bucket that fit her rear for late night disposal. We had to draw all our water from a hand dug well. It was about 20 feet deep and supplied plenty of water in the rainy season. During the hot summer months, we sometimes could only draw muddy water.

MEDICAL FACILITIES

Noble had no hospital and our nearest doctor was seven miles north in the village of Converse, LA. My mother used Dr. Murdock there for all her needs. They did not have the fancy machines back then, so they had no way of knowing a mother was carrying twins. My mother told other women how she thought she was deformed because she was so big. Roland was born and everybody was happy. Then the doctor called Dad about 15 minutes later and said he had another boy (me). Just teasing, the doctor called Dad again and said he had boys all over the delivery room. Dad almost fainted.

EARLY MEMORY

I can remember going to a hospital and Uncle Aleen putting me in scales to be weighed. The scales were rounded to fit a baby. We had to be about 2 years old. I also remember a drive to Converse hospital. The highway was gravel. Years later I asked about that road and they told me that Hwy 171 was gravel taken out from Cox hill.

MOVING TO TEXAS

In 1939 Dad got a job in Silsbee, TX, working for Kirby Lumber Company. He was very good at estimating the yield of a growth of timber. The big saw mills, such as Kirby, needed that kind of woods foreman who could estimate a track of timber. Dad worked in South Texas for many weeks before his company had a house for us to live in. I remember he would come home on the week-ends. Roe and I wanted to help on the expense of filling his gas tank. One week-end we filled up his gas tank with rocks and dry cow paddies (we were only about 2 years old). Needless to say, that was our first and last time to help out on the fuel. Side note: We never locked a car or home door at night in Noble.

THE TEXAS MOVE

I was I was riding with Uncle Aleen and Aunt L. J. on one of our trips to Texas. Someone had given them a syrup bucket full of fresh butter-milk and they were so proud of it. We had no cows in Texas so the butter-milk was like gold. They set it on the floor in the back of the little Ford. You guessed it; when I got in their car I stepped in the bucket of butter milk and it went all over me and the car. They were very nice about the spill but called me "Butter-Milk-Pete" from then on.

DARK-OUT NIGHTS

Our move to Texas was still during WW ll. Every night we had to block all light coming from our windows. Paper had to be pasted over all windows. Inspectors would come in your yard and if they saw a speck of light they would write you up. They said the enemy aircraft could see our light and may bomb our city. They had my attention.

COUSIN ONNIE WENT IN THE MARINES IN 1940

Roe and I were four years old in 1941. Onnie, my first cousin, was already in the Marines and was at the bombing at Pearl Harbor on Dec. 7th.

First report was that he was missing in action; later, the Red Cross said he was wounded, but would survive. A few months later he came home on a furlough. He recovered completely.

ARMY MANEUVERS IN NOBLE (1942)

The US Army had maneuvers in and all through Sabine Parish. Roe and I got to climb on tanks and half-tracks and learned what the word 'Buddy' meant. The Army boys called us Buddy. General Patton was in charge of the troops around Noble. He could be seen wearing the pearl handle 45 Cal. Pistols around town. They dug deep holes in the forest to bury their large artillery guns to make them secure. Many holes from their emplacements are still in the forest today.

ROE AND I HELPED WIN THE WAR

Roe and I gathered scrap-iron to help in the war effort. My mother, grand-mother, and aunt cooked homemade meals for a lot of the troops. They only charged what it cost them. The solders loved it. We could take in about 10 soldiers each evening. We also took in washing and ironing as a favor since the Army guys had no way to stay clean in the Louisiana woods. (Many of the solders had never been off the concrete of the large cities. The Redbugs and wasps had a field day on these poor troops.)

I remember they had many mock battles in our area. They had a Red Team and a Blue Team. The little airplanes would fly over and, for a bomb effect, they would drop a sack of flour. Of course it would explode and make a lot of white smoke. I loved watching the aerobatics. Maybe that is why I wanted to be a fighter pilot. And thank the Lord, He allowed me to fly fighter aircraft for the navy years later.

TWINS

Being raised as a twin was fun to say the least. It had advantages and disadvantages. But sometimes it was just down-right aggravating. We learned to swap names just to confuse people. People would gawk at us and say, "Here come the twins."

Cousin Onnie went on to become a civil engineer. We twins fared well and today enjoy fine lives in Texas. We will never forget the struggle and felt patriotism of those days.

Ron (LCDR USN) and Roe (MAJ USAF)

. . . .

We Malin Twins Did Our Part, Too!

The Knott Twins Were Not Alone

Bob and Dick Malin b. 1937

Having read Ron & Roland Knott's story, we have one too. Our mom had twin boys on Sept. 11, 1937. Like the Knott boys, the second one was not expected. Mom said she and Dad were very happy. I guess our older sister was too.

162

HOME FRONT

We remember the war years. It helped the war effort to produce your own food. We had a "victory garden" and got chickens that produced enough eggs for our family and some of our neighbors. We lived in Port Chester NY, not exactly farm country. After the war the neighbors wanted us to get rid of the chickens, so we had a lot of chicken dinners.

As a little kid, I had scary dreams of Japanese planes dropping bombs. I was afraid of my closet because I knew a spy could be in there! At night the fire whistle would blow and we would have to turn the lights out. We both went on to careers in the art field. We used to draw planes and tanks, etc. on wrapping paper in the war years. Most everything was rationed.

Our two uncles were in the war. Uncle George, our favorite, was in the Normandy invasion.(and survived). Uncle Bob was stationed in Iceland. Our Dad had a deferment because of having four kids and working at defense facilities.

Our Grandmother, MiMi, had a 41 Buick, with an allowance of four gallons of gas a week! All three of her daughters and all the kids piled into the Buick to do the food shopping. She whipped around a corner one time and we yelled out, "MiMi! Brian went out the door!" She was a lousy driver. Cousin Brian wasn't hurt. At school the kids bought war stamps and when you filled the books you got a war bond.

Xmas 1946

Bob and Dick with father Ed and sister Ginny

On VJ day we talked Dad into shooting the double barrel off the back porch. He did, both barrels at once. What fun! People were shooting guns and honking horns. A very happy day!

On to the post years, life was good. People were able to obtain things again; cars, metal goods, bubble gum, sneakers, etc. No more rationing, meatless Tuesdays,... on and on. Let's not forget.

. . . .

Making Rationing Work

'Making Do' Meant Working Together

Lyla K. b. 1936

Prices had been going up fast because of the shortages and then along came rationing. A lot of my memories about those times have to do with all the hitches and squabbles in our big family about rationing and hoarding and swapping rationing stickers. They changed over to tokens and points and we had to learn about when things expired. Some stores would let you trade one kind of stamp for another. One store in our town was like a bank with lots of tokens, points, stickers and ration books. Some people said it was illegal. Ads in the newspapers said, "Don't pay above the ceiling price!" I worried when I overheard that one of my aunts had bought meat on the black market because my teacher said you could go to jail.

What I remember are the times when our neighbors and my mother and her sisters would all get together in our kitchen and talk in loud voices about rationing. They argued a lot about who owed what from last time and who would get extra next time. The stamps, tokens and checks did not all come on the same day or expire at the same time and that made things complicated. But they always worked things out and they always said they could 'make do'. Which everybody said.

....

Some Fun on the Home Front

These Signs Also Helped Keep Us Safe

George Terranova, MD b. 1943

For those who never saw any of the Burma Shave signs, here is a quick lesson in a different aspect of our 'Home Front.'

Before there were interstates, when everyone drove the old two lane roads, Burma Shave signs would be posted all over the countryside in farmers' fields. They were small red signs with white letters. Five signs, about 100 feet apart, each containing one line of a four line couplet... and the obligatory 5th sign advertising Burma Shave, a popular shaving cream.

DON'T STICK YOUR ELBOW
OUT SO FAR
IT MAY GO HOME
IN ANOTHER CAR. Burma Shave

TRAINS DON'T WANDER
ALL OVER THE MAP
'CAUSE NOBODY SITS
IN THE ENGINEER'S LAP. Burma Shave

SHE KISSED THE HAIRBRUSH
BY MISTAKE
SHE THOUGHT IT WAS
HER HUSBAND JAKE. Burma Shave

DON'T LOSE YOUR HEAD
TO GAIN A MINUTE
YOU NEED YOUR HEAD
YOUR BRAINS ARE IN IT. Burma Shave

DROVE TOO LONG
DRIVER SNOOZING
WHAT HAPPENED NEXT
IS NOT AMUSING. Burma Shave

BROTHER SPEEDER

LET'S REHEARSE
ALL TOGETHER
GOOD MORNING, NURSE. Burma Shave

CAUTIOUS RIDER
TO HER RECKLESS DEAR
LET'S HAVE LESS BULL
AND A LITTLE MORE STEER. Burma Shave

SPEED WAS HIGH
WEATHER WAS NOT
TIRES WERE THIN
X MARKS THE SPOT. Burma Shave

THE MIDNIGHT RIDE
OF PAUL FOR BEER
LED TO A WARMER
HEMISPHERE. Burma Shave

AROUND THE CURVE
LICKETY-SPLIT
BEAUTIFUL CAR
WASN'T IT? Burma Shave

NO MATTER THE PRICE
NO MATTER HOW NEW
THE BEST SAFETY DEVICE
IN THE CAR IS YOU. Burma Shave

A GUY WHO DRIVES
A CAR WIDE OPEN
IS NOT THINKIN' HE'S JUST HOPIN'. Burma Shave

AT INTERSECTIONS
LOOK EACH WAY
A HARP SOUNDS NICE
BUT IT'S HARD TO PLAY. Burma Shave

BOTH HANDS ON THE WHEEL
EYES ON THE ROAD
THAT'S THE SKILLFUL
DRIVER'S CODE. Burma Shave

THE ONE WHO DRIVES

WHEN HE'S BEEN DRINKING
DEPENDS ON YOU
TO DO HIS THINKING. Burma Shave

CAR IN DITCH
DRIVER IN TREE
THE MOON WAS FULL
AND SO WAS HE. Burma Shave

PASSING SCHOOL ZONE
TAKE IT SLOW
LET OUR LITTLE
SHAVERS GROW. Burma Shave

....

Carolina Home Front

From Small Town to a Life in the Air

Don Parker b. 1934

I was born in 1934 on a small farm in a small northeastern North Carolina town, Murfreesboro, population about 1200. Iit was a rural farming community about 45 miles from Norfolk, Virginia. Looking back, it was wonderful, as life was uncomplicated and I fit the profile of everyone else who had a similar beginning: Saturday movie westerns, usually a double feature, plus the great "continueds" Captain Marvel, Dick Tracy, Don

C. D. PETERSON

Winslow of the Navy, Green Hornet, and of course Superman and Bat Man.

Our parents were products of the depression......strict and caring. We moved into town in 1941 when I was seven. My father built a house and I remember him saying that it would take a very long time to pay for it - the total cost was $5500 including the lot. It still stands today.

Our school was in a three story building about 1000 yards from our home and I walked to school every day. The first and second grade was 1/2 below ground so from our chairs we could see the feet and legs of everyone who was outside through the windows. The cafeteria was on that level. Grades three through seven were on the second floor and grades eight through twelve were on the third floor. Stairs only. We had excellent teachers. I even had a teacher who had taught my father many years before when they only had one room for the whole school. She taught math and Latin and was one tough cookie.

In those years following Pearl Harbor, until early 1946, life changed for us in what we had or could get via the rationing program which included most everything. It was put into place for just about everything that you needed soon after Dec. 7th. But being seven years old was still rather uncomplicated.

Being so close to Norfolk and the huge Naval presence we had many blackouts and air raid drills. We had an airplane spotter shack right in the middle of town and it was manned during daylight all the time. I used to sit after school with the men who manned it and when an airplane would come overhead the spotter would have to attempt to identify it as best he could and call someone in Norfolk and give a report with his best estimate. The direction of flight was very important.

German POW's worked in the fields and I remember they had military clothing. We would ride our bicycles out to where they were working and they would wave at us and we could hear them laughing and talking. We were in total awe.

We had, as did all of the small towns, all the sports programs like basketball, baseball, football and of course inter mural of everything - if you could find enough people who wanted to participate. As I remember, most everyone had a "Letter" in something, not that they were necessarily that good but they were all who were available.

Everybody-and I mean everybody- was a Democrat, which looking back, I remember the adults talking politics on Sunday afternoon while sipping iced tea and, as I recall, I would now assess their philosophy as having a strong conservative belief somewhere between General Mattis and

168

Rand Paul. Self sufficient, strong Christian belief, a keen sense of community and great pride and most were of high moral character and integrity.

Boy Scouts were a big thing at 12, and I took it seriously and earned 32 merit badges. I never made Eagle Scout because I couldn't swim and you had to have the Lifesaving Merit badge to get it. I made Life Scout, however, and I have always regretted not being able to become an Eagle Scout. Such is life I suppose. We had about 20 Scouts and we had a great time doing all the things Scouts do. The Scout Master was home from the Navy and the War and had the biggest influence on me because he was a Navy pilot. I had known him as a neighbor three doors away when he went in the Navy in 1942.

After the war, he made arrangements with the Navy at his Reserve unit in Norfolk bring the entire Scout troop to Norfolk for his drill weekend. We arrived and they assigned a 1st class Petty Officer to be with us from Friday afternoon until Sunday. We had an agenda of planned activities which, as far as I was concerned, put me in heaven or as close to it as I would ever get. We even each got to fly in a

TBM simulator. (It actually was a Link trainer but they told us it was a TBM.) The Navy treated us royally and, as I look back at it, what fantastic PR for the impressionable minds we all were. Sunday afternoon the final event was..... we all piled into the back of a P5M seaplane and they flew us around Norfolk and Virginia Beach for almost an hour returning for a water landing and a talk from the pilot. There had never been any doubt about what I wanted to do, but this sealed the package.

I was in the 7th grade and kept that enthusiasm from then on. That was 1947. I finished college at Univ of North Carolina in 1955 and as fast as I could get to the US Navy I did. I had taken the tests during my senior year and the physical just before June, so I went to Norfolk and I was in. The recruiter gave me a ride in an SNJ and told me it would be the last free ride. He did all the acrobatics he knew and I was in total heaven. They shipped me to Pensacola on a train, which was my first train ride ever, for Class 19-55. Most all you know what happened after that, as your life was taken over by the Navy. I enjoyed every minute of the training.

The single most surprising thing that ever happened to me took place two or three weeks before we were to finish the 16 weeks of pre-flight and head out to Basic. The Battalion Commander, Captain Lewendowski, had instructed the Sgt. to call out all in the class who had finished college and had a degree. I believe that there were about 10 or 12 of us and we went to his office wondering "what now ?"

He had a document in his hand and he proceeded to read it to us telling us that the Navy was instituting a new program that would give us a commission upon graduation from pre-flight which was 2 weeks away. The class in front of us, Class 18, would be the first and we would be the second. He congratulated us and we left his office speechless. It happened that way and of course it became known as the AOC program and as far as I know still exists.

So, we finished as Ensign's and it did make a great life even greater. The downside was that we, like us all, had formed a close bond with all the guys in Class 19, but then we separated and went our separate ways for the rest of training.

Many years later, in early 1990's, one of the guys got together with USAA and they mailed a letter to everyone who was still insured by them telling them that we were going to attempt a reunion for Class 19-55 at Pensacola. He got an excellent response and we did in fact meet there for a few days. Through a real happenstance we found the DI, Sgt. Paul Haynes, and he and his wife attended. We subsequently got together each year for several years and we still communicate regularly. Great bunch of guys !

I left the Navy in 1959 to American Airlines got laid off in late 1960. I went back into the Navy at Corpus Christi as a flight instructor in P2V's

. . . .

for 2 years in VT-31. I returned to American at the end of 1962 and remained there until retirement in 1994. CV 240, DC-6. DC-7, L-188, BAC-111, B-727, B-757, B-767.

Do it all over?............YES!

The Villain in Our Childhood

Not all memories about this era make me smile.

C. D. Peterson b. 1937

A villain lurked in all our childhoods back then. We talked about the villain, but always in quiet tones. We worried because we didn't know when he might strike or who might be stricken next. We heard he could strike when you took a drink at the water fountain in the Hollis Theater or went swimming in Learned's Pond. Parents couldn't protect you. Nothing could protect you from polio.

One Saturday morning before we went to the movies, a bunch of us went to see a boy who was in an iron lung because he had polio. He lived on a nice tree lined street near Butterworth Field, where we played baseball. We lined up in silence and walked single file through the house to a quiet, front living room. All I could see was his head lying on a pillow, sticking out from the round cylinder of a machine that made hissing sounds.

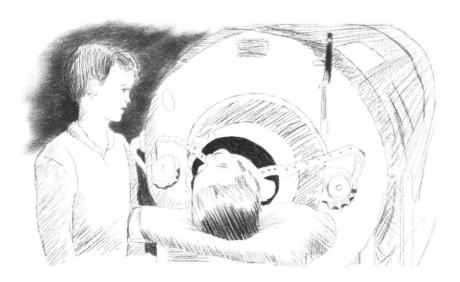

171

He had dark hair, and I didn't know his name, but I said "hello" and he said "hello" back. He was smiling. His mother followed us out and called to us as we walked away, "It was very nice of you boys to come by. It's not contagious, you know. Come back again." I had never had so much as a cold and couldn't imagine what that boy must have been feeling. I became sad every time I thought about him lying there, trapped in that steel tube, not able to be outside.

They were great times, but let's remember they were not perfect.

. . . .

A Boy's Home Front - from Miami

Pearl Harbor, saving stamps and oleo

H. C. 'Nick' Nickerson b. 1935

In 1941 I was six years old, and although I remember Christmas that year, no one made me aware of the bombing of Pearl Harbor three weeks before. I'm sure they were trying to shelter me from the horror of the attack, but I've always regretted that my parents didn't alert me to the significance of that day.

Nick in 1940

In the early 40s, anything that cost a dollar was an expensive item. I do remember a neighbor lady complaining to my mother that a trip to the

grocery store cost almost twenty dollars. For that matter I do remember my mom sending me to the local neighborhood grocery with eleven cents to buy a loaf of bread.

During those days, I remember a horse drawn wagon coming through the neighborhood selling fresh vegetables. (I wonder now how that worked with food rationing going on.) Another entrepreneur would come by offering to sharpen knives and scissors. Paper drives were in vogue. I never quite knew what they did with old newspapers and magazines, but it seemed very important. We donated any metal utensils and old pots and pans. We saved bacon and other kitchen grease for the war effort and turned our collection into the local butcher. They told us it would be used in manufacturing ammunition.

Rationing took away our butter. We were able to get white oleo margarine where they attached a packet of yellow food coloring you had to add to make it look like butter. Some 'oleo' had a colored bubble inside and you kneaded it for several minutes to spread the color around. I understand it was the dairy industry who demanded no margarine could look like butter. Mom would let me stir up the mixture.

Gasoline rationing was in place. Our family car had a B sticker which allowed us to purchase a little more gas than the A sticker. I guess it was because of Dad's job with Pan American. My Uncle Dick had an A sticker. I don't remember what he did for a living. He had a 1934 Ford coupe with a rumble seat where I got to ride sometimes. He and Aunt Henrietta lived in downtown Miami. He was an Air Raid Warden and patrolled the

Nick in 1944

streets around his apartment during black outs to ensure no unauthorized lights were showing. He wore a white helmet showing his badge of office. He was very proud of that.

Automobiles had the upper half of their headlights shaded. Along Miami Beach all windows had heavy shades installed and were drawn at night. This precluded any background lights from illuminating the tankers and cargo ships traveling just off shore in the Gulf Stream. This procedure surely helped stop the massive sinking by German submarines in the early months of the war.

Dad became a navigator with Pan American during the war years, delivering medium bombers to Russia via the Caribbean, South America, Africa, and the Near East. He flew out of Opa Locka Airport in North Miami. One evening, Mom put us in the car and drove over to the airport's perimeter fence and parked to watch Dad take-off. Soon, an armed sentry came by and told us to move on. Parking there was not allowed for security.

Mom got a wartime job with the Government. I remember she took a bus every morning to Homestead Army Air Field. I don't remember what her job was.

War Bonds were a big thing during the war. Kids were encouraged to buy Savings Stamps, some for 10 cents, some for 25 cents.

The kids had stamp books in which the stamps were pasted. When you had $18.75 you could purchase a War Bond that matured for $25 ten years later.

At age ten in 1945, we were told at school President Roosevelt died. Walking home after school that afternoon with some other children, we discussed the possibility that we might now lose the war with him gone. Childhood fears at their best!

At the war's end, Dad left Pan Am, and Mom left her job in Homestead and became a bookkeeper at the Dade County Court House. I went on to Miami Jackson High School and my sister, Patsy finished up at Miami High. We moved to Fort Lauderdale in 1950, and I went on to graduate from Fort Lauderdale High School in 1953.

. . . .

Time Flys

RECOLLECTIONS: 1941 - 1955

Stephen B. Miller B. 1934

I was seven years old in 1941, living in a suburb of Cincinnati, Ohio but had no inkling of war-related issues and constraints at that time. My dad died in 1941. Mom was an accomplished legal secretary and supported my younger sister and me.

Around 1944 we moved to a Miami Beach apartment where mom worked as J.C. Penney's private secretary. He transported her to and from his mansion every day in a limo. Kids of my age were free to roam the area at will in those days. No drug problem existed then. We'd play various types of hide 'n seek games on the rooftops of nearby homes until well after dark. Mom was a good swimmer and had a special pool pass so we also did that fairly often. Only once did the evidence of war show up. One day at the beach I saw a submarine a few hundred yards offshore chasing a PT boat which was trying to get away from it. Suddenly there was a flash and "boom" from the sub's deck gun followed by a near-miss spray near the PT boat. For a moment I wondered "Is this a movie, or what?" I finally realized that this was a German U-boat firing at one of our PT boats!

Busy as she was, mom took me to a small airport once, where I had a ride in an Ercoupe. I knew then that aviation was for me! Mom was then going with my stepdad, who was in the Army in North Africa. After the war ended, I can still remember going down to the train station to pick him up, still in uniform and carrying his duffel bag.

Around 1947 we moved back to Cincinnati, though I can't remember exactly when mom and pop were married. We became close with his family and acquired many new relatives. My newfound cousins and I were into model airplanes and the usual dogfight simulations, always cognizant of the latest military aircraft. We were mesmerized each evening when the Stinson Reliant mail plane flew over the house.

Over the next few years, by the time I graduated from college in 1955, I had worked at the local (Lunken) airport, learned to fly at age 16 at a small airport.

Eventually I became a Naval Aviator, flying AD-5N's off the U.S.S. Essex (CVA9) in the 1950's (cold war).

The house I returned to in Cincinnati was intentionally burned down by the fire department decades ago. A Pizza hut sits there now. Likewise, the Essex, my old aircraft carrier, has long since turned to scrap. I may have shaved with parts of it in my razor blades.

It's hard to believe all the changes in my life during the 1940's - 1950's!

....

The Wyoming Home Front

War changes come inland

Anonymous b. 1937

I recall my father and grandfather discussing the bombing of Pearl Harbor in December 1941, but at four years of age I did not comprehend the significance of it. Being so far inland, we were never subject to black outs and, although the town siren sounded every day at noon, I do not recall any air raid drills such as I have read about in major cities.

My parents started saving tinfoil and I can remember peeling it off of chewing gum wrappers, and some candy wrappers. A sign was erected in a small park on Main Street that listed the names of the men that were in service.

My mother and my grandmother had large "Victory Gardens," but the change was lost on me as we had always had pretty big vegetable gardens. I recall discussions about rationing and my parents using honey rather than sugar as a sweetener in their coffee.

The USAAF built an airfield outside of Casper, Wyoming, about 25 miles west of my hometown. It opened in late 1942 and trained crews for both B24s and B17s. A part of that facility was a target range for practice bombing and gunnery. That range was located about 15 miles north of my hometown in a scrub brush, sand hill area. As a result, men in uniform and Army vehicles became a common sight in our little town.

The range crews drove back and forth from the air base and the range every day, and became regulars at the local establishments such as the bars, the lone movie theater and grocery stores. A few even became overnight guests in the one cell city jail.

176

As more crews trained at Casper crashes became inevitable and were fairly common. A history[1] of the base shows that "Over one hundred forty Casper Army Air Base aviators perished in 90 plane crashes between September 1942 and March 1945." **(see the link below)**

I recall my dad taking me to a crash site near the bombing range and seeing the wreckage of the airplane.

There was an USO Canteen in Casper and many of the young women from our town went to entertain at that Canteen. That is where my aunt met her husband to be. It was probably late 1943 or early 1944 as he had completed his required combat missions as a tail gunner in B24 Liberators in North Africa. He was assigned to the Casper USAAF Airfield as a gunnery instructor.

= The Author's uncle Homer (a B24 gunner) his father Dale, his grandfather Manley, and his great uncle George.

Shortly after he and my aunt started dating, he incurred lung damage from an inflight fire during one of the training missions. The damage was severe enough that in 1944 he was medically discharged and he and my aunt were married.

http://www.wyohistory.org/encyclopedia/aerials-zephyrs-brief-history-casper-army-air-base

. . . .

A Boy's Home Front - 1940's Oglesby, Illinois

A Boy's Home Front in the Mid 1940's

James Duncan b.1941

Oglesby, a sleepy little farm town in the midst of vast fields of corn. Northern Illinois about 100 miles southwest of Chicago. No interstate, no supercenters, TV or cell towers. Nickel movies on Saturday afternoons. Tom Mix, Three Stooges and war time news reels (remember the narrators voice?). Yo-Yo contests at intermission. Mine had rhinestones and could "walk the dog".

Sunday nights in front of the floor model Philco. The Shadow, Amos n Andy and Fibber McGee.

Living with Dad's parents, Tudie and Pa. Mean cocker spaniel named Bunny. Don't stick your finger in the kitchen door crack. Bunny would and did bite. Mom hated Bunny. Six people, one bath, steam hot water, lump coal furnace. Take out the clinker ash. Dinner was noon. Pa takes nap and goes back to his lumber yard. Sandwiches at night. Lard bucket on back stoop. Cook everything in lard. Save lard. Use it again. Tudie picks concord grapes in back arbor. Squeeze them in cloth bags. Catch juice and make jelly. Melt paraffin and pour over jars. Cool and seal.

Washington Park two houses down. Swings, merry go round, monkey bars and metal slides. No rubber mats or crushed tire mulch. Skinned knees, splinters bumps and bruises. Play through it. World War 1 cannon also in park.. Two big wheels. Shimmy up barrel and hang down. Green Schwinn fat tire bike with Bendix brakes. Band concert shell with concerts on summer Saturday nights. Men just getting home from war. John Phillip Sousa. Glenn Miller sounds. Popcorn balls two for a nickel.

Pa and I walking Bunny after dark. I sneak off to Bobby's house and go to Ben Franklin with parents. Arrive home an hour later. Confronted by Pa. My chin in his large hand. He is shaking. No more of that.

Doc Rock lives three door away. Very bulbous nose and thick glasses. Think Dickens. He birthed all three of us kids and removed my appendix and tonsils. What's a specialist? Would walk down to Pa's house with black back any time. Like to have cocktails with Pa. Christmas eves at Rocks. Hot egg nog. Santa would pound on front door with great fanfare. Smelled like bourbon.

Leave house summer mornings to find the day's adventure. Back at noon. Summoned by bell on back porch. Out again. No helicopter mom or name for free range parents. No political with correct in same sentence yet. Forbidden to go down to Vermillion River. Sure. Cross street into

178

Jim Duncan with mother and sister on 4th of July 1949.

woods. Down hill past old coal mine buildings. Great place to play war. Over the slag heaps (red ash) left from mines. Arrive at narrow fast moving Vermillion. Skip rocks, look for stuff and critters. Watch the bucket tram carry limestone from the quarry on the other side to the cement mill. (Where I would work four summers in college).

Home filthy and tired. Sandwich, bath and to bed. Mom, Dad and sister in room to the right. Tudie and Pa each in separate bedrooms. His very large. Do not go in there. Bunny locked in kitchen. Prayers on knees. Nod off to sounds on hoot owl family quietly vocalizing and the nightly steam engine train revving up to make the grade to the mill. I think I can…. I think I can.

Yes we can and we did.

. . . .

A War Time Memory

A War Time Memory – My Train Ride

Donald Rogers b. 1935

In 1941 when my grandmother died, my father bought the 77 acre farm from his siblings and we moved from Tampa to Mayfield, Kentucky.

Our house in Kentucky, where my father had grown up, was without electricity and lacked indoor plumbing for about the first year, as I remember. Our house was heated by a fireplace and portable oil heaters.

We survived growing most of our food on the farm. We did not have a car initially and made the three mile trip to Mayfield in a wagon pulled by horses.

I entered school in the second grade. My school did not have indoor plumbing facilities. Many Sundays were spent with church families after dinner – our noon meal. We consumed a lot of chicken and pork along with banana pudding when ingredients were available. Bananas were in limited supply along with pineapple, sugar, washing powder, and gasoline. Ladies used feed sacks for making dresses.

While we were living in Kentucky my mother and I made numerous trips back to Florida on trains from Fulton, Kentucky to Tampa. Many soldiers and sailors were traveling on the trains then. They smoked and laughed but their eyes were sad.

The "Seminole" was steam engine powered and always late and crowded with passengers. The "City of Miami," which traveled from Chicago to Miami, was powered by a diesel engine.

My memorable train ride happened when a train conductor took me up to the engine and I met the engineer. There I was, riding up in the engine of the "City of Miami" through the Alabama mountains at night!

. . . .

A Boy's Chicago Home Front

War Time Farming - Chicago Style

Jim Kelly b. 1935

Growing up in Chicago during the war, every empty lot became a victory garden. We kids would sneak in at night & eat veggies. We saved ripe tomatoes for missiles.

. . . .

The Post war home front changes

Change Didn't Take Too Long

Dr. Donald Gardner b. 1945

I grew up in he 50's and attended St. Brenden's Grammar school in the Bronx, N.Y.from 1949 until we left for the suburbs of N.J. in 1959.

I remember wearing dog tags and having practice air-raid drills and by being "protected" under my desk from a Russian nuclear attack.

I also remember a much safer time, earlier, right after the war, when I was able to walk home from St. Brenden's for 6 blocks by myself, before my mother would meet me at the corner of Decatur Ave. and Gun Hill Road. I was only 5 and in kindergarten the first year.

. . . .

The Civil Air Patrol on the Home Front
Colonel Bob Mosely b. 1924

(Brother of Zack Mosely, creator of the popular comic strip "Smilin' Jack")

The Civil Air Patrol (CAP) had been given a mission by the US Army Air Forces to perform shore patrol duties off the Fla. coast from Palm Beach up north to Cape Canaveral (about 130 miles of coast) and then there was another CAP unit out of Miami for the area south of us and others on up the north coasts, all the way to Maine (as I remember it). German submarines by that time were sinking many cargo ships along the east coast. The Gulf Stream is a current of water about 50 miles wide (just a guess) and moves at about 10 to 15 knots and flows around the bottom of Fla. out of the Gulf of Mexico and north along the coast and then on out into the Atlantic.

The US ships moving south would often get in very close to shore, to get inside the Gulf Stream and avoid the current so as to not lose that 10 to 15 knots of speed. At this time the Army Air Forces were short on planes and could not provide much in the way of patrol coverage. And if a submarine was spotted by some other source, a call would have to be made through channels and a very slow observation plane could then be dispatched, but if the observation plane did not happen to be in that particular area at that, it might have to come all the way down from Savannah Georgia. This was obviously no threat to the Germans so they were having a field day out there sinking merchant ships.—When the ships were in so close to land, inside the Gulf Stream, the Germans would silhouette them against the lights of Palm beach at night and blaze away at them (this led to more strict blackout rules). They were in so close we were awakened several nights (living in West Palm Beach) by torpedo explosions sinking ships. Some of the broken hulls stayed around for a long time; one in particular off of Vero Beach was visible for as much as 20 years later.

These sinkings led to a bunch a things; one being a lot of oil on the beaches, one being a total black out at nights (we had to tape up the head lights of our cars and leave only a little slit of light for night driving, but with gas rationing there wasn't all that much driving going on anyhow) and another thing it brought about was the change in the mission of the CAP being upgraded from an observation/rescue role to a more aggressive role, to try to help out with the German submarine menace. The idea was to put 100 pound bombs on the little Stinson 10 A, 90 HP planes we flew. Now we really did not expect to do a lot of damage with those little planes, although they could possibly inflict some damage. But, mainly it was figured that the Germans had some kind of electronic gear to detect an airplane was over head, and it might deter an attack.

With the advent of the beginning of the war, that sleepy little airport in West Palm Beach that I had fallen in love with when I arrived in West Palm Beach in 1940, became Morrison Field and a bee hive of activity with military planes of all sorts parked everywhere. Thus, there was no room for any civilian operations like there had been for the original Florida Air Patrol and early CAP operations, so the CAP operations had to be moved to the new Lantana airport, about 5 miles to the south of West Palm Beach.

It was at this time, thanks to my brother, Zack, that I got into the CAP as a pilot because I had my pilots license. I went from a grunt working 10 hours a day, 6 days a week, for $10 dollars—washing, fueling and hangaring airplanes—to a Second Lieutenant in the CAP, where they paid me $8 dollars a day and I could get all of the flying time I wanted. They called that pay Per Diem; a word I came very familiar with later on in my career. I had definitely moved up in the world and I was beginning to realize that my decision to become a military pilot; i.e. work for the Government, was not a bad idea from a monetary stand point as well as getting to fly their beautiful airplanes.

I really loved that CAP experience. For as mentioned before, nearly all of those Civil Air Patrol pilots were of Zack's age or older (a couple of them had even been in World War One). They were successful people by my standards in that they had made enough money to buy their own planes, and also they were very experienced pilots. I had enormous respect for them and it was an honor to get to fly with such men. They seemed to respect me also even though I had done nothing to prove myself except that I did have a pilot'+s license. Part of their respect for me, I'm sure, came from the fact that I was Zack's brother. But I suspect it also was the fact that they knew I was going to be getting in the real shooting war very soon and they were too old and would not be able to get to do that. That is a strange thing to think about as I write this, in that people really wanted to go to war which could mean getting killed. But a person needed to have lived at that time, when your country was really in danger of being taken over by the Germans and the Japanese, to understand how Americans wanted to get in the fight. It was an extremely threatening period and almost everyone wanted to do their part.

Bob Mosley and Brother Zack Taxi for 1942 CAP Flight

We wore a uniform that looked very similar to a regular US Army Air Forces uniform except the wings were different and we had red epaulets which attracted so much attention that I never wore the uniform except when I had to. This wasn't so much from a pride stand point even though the red epaulets did create some giggles. It was mainly because I had not yet earned my military wings and I didn't want anyone to think I was trying to impersonate a military pilot.

As stated before, the airplane we used primarily was the 90 Horsepower Stinson 10A. Our coastal patrol mission was pretty much the same each time we flew. We would take off from the Lantana airport in a very loaded condition (maximum gas load, a 100 pound bomb, and emergency equipment) which made you wonder on some of those hot days whether you were going to make it off at all because the runway was not very long and that little Stinson loved the ground. There were always two pilots and in back of the seats was space for the emergency equipment which consisted of some flares, our flotation equipment (a deflated car inner tube) with a canvas sack attached to it. This was referred to as the "Barracuda Bucket". The idea was that if you had to ditch, after hopefully surviving the water landing, you would be able to get out of the plane then swim back and go into the back seat of the plane and drag out the Barracuda Bucket. You were then to inflate the inner tube (while swimming) with a small bicycle pump that was back there also. Hopefully, then you could get into the middle of the inner tube and lower yourself, part way at least, down into the sack. I don't know whether it was ever successfully used or not; I personally doubted it's practicality. We did wear Mae Wests though and I was a good swimmer, so the only thing I hoped for if I had to ditch was to survive the landing and get out of the plane. I figured I could take it from there.

Getting back to the mission, we nearly always took off to the east and there was a small lake right at the end of the runway. Across the lake were trees and a few houses. The lake was longer north and south than it was east and west though, so on those hot days when there was doubt that you were going to clear the trees across the lake going straight ahead east, we would get airborne as soon as the plane felt like flying, then cautiously bank over the lake and head north up the lake until we could get some more airspeed.

You were also operating over a cooler surface over the lake than when you were on the runway, so the plane began to perform a little better and thus you could clear the trees at the north end of the lake with no problems. We would then head out due east over the ocean to about 10 miles off shore and then zig-zag for the next 4 hours on a northerly course. This would put us about 40 miles out from the coast by the time we were abreast of the Banana River Naval Air Station, just south of Cape Canaveral because the coast of Fla. runs at about 160-340 degrees. What we were actually doing was tracking pretty much along with the Gulf Stream which slowly pulls away from the coast as it heads north from the Palm Beach area. Now, 40 miles doesn't sound like much but you can't see land from that distance at 1000 feet and with only a single engine aircraft it is a long way to swim if that one engine quits. We would then turn west and go in and land at the Banana River Naval Air Station (now Patrick Air Force Base) and get some gas and then turn around and do a search pattern back down the coast for another 4 hours; just the reverse of what we had done coming north. There would also be another patrol taking off from Lantana as we would be heading back, thus we pretty well kept a plane out there all the time. The last flight of the day would spend the night at the Banana River Naval Air station and then we would get up real early and be ready for take off at dawn. I certainly had no intuition that the Banana River Naval Air Station, i.e. Patrick Air Force Base and it's environs would play such an important part in the later years of my life.

I had only one bad experience in all of that flying over the ocean (probably 2 to 3 hundred hours) other than having to fly around and through those summer afternoon thunder storms. It happened on a Sunday afternoon about 30 miles off the coast of Vero Beach and I was flying with one of "Zack's old hillbilly friends", Zeke Cornelius (they were not hill billies but their names sounded like they were), i.e., Zeke, Zack, Jake, and Ike. We were just cruising along as nice as you please at 1000 feet when suddenly the engine started getting rough and then real rough. The engine cowling looked like it was moving up and down about 4 inches and if we had crashed I would have told everyone that the engine must have come loose from it's mounts. We checked everything we could think of which was not all that much, but we were losing our 1000 feet rapidly.

I had already accepted the fact that we were going to ditch and we headed toward the nearest freighter in sight and started making MAYDAY calls, Then Zeke thought of one other thing to try and that was to switch from both magnetos to the 'left only' magneto then to the 'right only' magneto. Going to the left magneto did no good but when he switched to the right magneto the engine smoothed out, and while at a little less than normal power, it was enough to pull us up from hitting the water and we limped in to the coast and landed at Vero Beach. I was told later that what had happened was a timing wheel/gear had come loose on the left magneto and it was causing a misfire in the cylinders; i.e., one magneto was fighting the other and the explosions were out of synch thus the violent roughness (at least that is the way the problem was explained to me). I can certainly vouch for the violence and I never had anything like that happen in all of the many hours I flew reciprocating engines in the years to follow.

Zeke and I went to a hotel in Vero Beach and spent the night. He was really shaken up and had to have a few drinks to settle down. I didn't drink in those days but I didn't really need anything anyhow because it didn't bother me all that much. However, if Zeke hadn't switched the mags when he did I would sure have had plenty to be bothered about by that time, because I probably would have still been out there trying to get the "Barracuda Bucket" out of the plane. There were no more exciting events in the remaining months that I flew with the patrol.

After I left the patrol all of the pilots were awarded the Air Medal for their daring flying out there over the ocean in single engine planes looking for German submarines.

I flew with the CAP until I was called into the Aviation cadet training in March of 1943. I was told after I departed that our Squadron had one airplane make a forced landing on the beach and one made a forced landing in the water, a short way off of the beach. There were no casualties in either case.

. . . .

A young life gets direction

I was inspired on a Sunday morning

Dave Pace b. 1934

In 1944 I was 10 years old. One Sunday morning I was at home in Leaksville, NC - now called by the nicer name Eden - waiting for my sister and brother to walk to Sunday School. The skies were clear but for a few a few puffy white clouds. From out of nowhere roared a Lockheed Lightening P-38 at chimney top level! It must have sent a "million" volts up my spine. The war was on, and I said to myself, "I'm going to do that some day."

Well, I did - and that's another story.

. . . .

VIEWING AN ECLIPSE

... AND REMEMBERING AN ECLIPSE

Anonymous b. 1937

The total eclipse event in 2017 brought back memories of my first viewing of a solar eclipse. This year's path of totality will cross my home town, Glenrock, in central Wyoming.

In 1939 the Great Depression was in full swing and my father had trouble finding work He had been injured in an accident while working for a pipeline company and had crushed his fingers on one hand. Being unable to work right away, he lost his job with the company. He then worked at whatever jobs he could find.

In 1940 my maternal grandfather, who lived in Oklahoma, said there was a large construction job in Tulsa that was short of laborers. With that, my parents loaded up my younger brother, me and whatever clothes they might need, into their car and headed south. Dad was able to get on the payroll there and we moved in with my mother's sister. But when the construction was complete, there were no jobs to be found in Oklahoma so my parents headed back to Wyoming.

They arrived back in Wyoming in early 1941, just as the CONOCO refinery in my home town was expanding and hiring new employees. Dad

My brother Gary (L) and me, about 1943

was able to get one of the jobs and remained with the company until 1955 when the refinery was closed.

Thus, in April 1941 we were resettled in our home and, according to Dad, things were looking up. *All of the above is based on conversations with my father, because I was three when we were in Oklahoma and my memories of that time are very few.*

However, my memory is pretty strong about many events that happened after returning to the place of my birth. One of the most distinct is about viewing the solar eclipse from our backyard. It was a partial eclipse where we lived, but my parents still made a big deal out of it. Dad had gotten some very dark glass, possibly out of a welder's mask, and I remember looking at the sun through that dark glass. My Dad's parents lived next door and they joined us to see it.

Of course at the time I did not realize the significance of the event but the memory remains with me to this day.

. . . .

Then and now

My fears back then seem so small now

Lucia O'Hara b. 1946

I read with interest all the descriptions of the differences in our lives from then and now. I was born in 1946 and did live in an all-family focused family. I can remember when I was in my late teens, I came home from being out and about, and my parents were not home. It seemed a crucial blow, even though they were simply at my grandparents' house playing cards! But to me it was my very first realization that they had a life separate from me. That's how safe I had always felt.

Yes, the cold war was always hanging over us back then, but today's burdens – the fear of terrorism and the sense of societal decay - seem to be much more overwhelming.

. . . .

Three excerpts from <u>We Were Not Spoiled</u> *by* **Lucille Ledoux** *as told to* **Denis Ledoux.**

HOME FRONT

1. Life During The War

By Lucille Ledoux b. 1921

Life during the war went on as usual, in some ways. I enjoyed working at Benoit's Clothing Store. I liked dressing up to go to work. We were always meeting the public and we had to look good. Our dresses had to be just right and our hair done. I used to go to a hairdresser on Lincoln Street whose shop was on the second floor of a building her family owned. She lived downstairs with her parents, who had made the second floor available to her for use as a beauty shop. Today, people would say you have to have a shop on the first floor.

Most days, I would take the bus back for lunch, which my mother prepared. The trip up took ten minutes and the bus left me right in front of our house. I'd eat for a half hour. Then, I'd pick the bus up in front, and the trip back took minutes.

After having had twelve children, my mother did not have any more. Paul was still very young—four in 1943—and Roger was six. My mother was quite busy. During this time, certainly by 1943, she was not doing too well, but we didn't think much of it. We continued to think of her as a strong woman.

That year, as the war was going on, I had a normal life. I served as president of les Enfants de Marie and met with other young women to prepare events to support Holy Family Church and its ministry. I also remember planting dahlias around the house. It was like planting little potatoes and getting beautiful flowers. In the fall, you had to dig them up and save them for the next season. It was a lot of work but I enjoyed doing it.

Many workplaces offered the option of having money taken from your pay to buy war bonds. The money was used by the US government to finance the war. I decided to join the effort and had money taken out regularly from my Benoit's pay. It was a patriotic thing to do and, since Albert and many other young men I knew were in the war, I felt I was doing something to support them. It was also a way of saving money because the bonds were supposed to be redeemable with some interest after the war was over.

By then, I had definitely begun to think that I might marry Albert. Because the war was going on, these were not easy years to be thinking of getting married. Not just being married but what happened after you married—starting a family and raising children. Every week, we read in the

English and the French newspapers that some young man had been killed, leaving a widow who was pregnant or a widow with children. That would be hard on the woman and hard on the children. All that year, Albert was in Keesler Army Air Force Base. He had gone through Mississippi's easy winter and then through its hot humid summer. He was slated to graduate from the program in December 1943. We knew nothing beyond that.

For more information, click here <u>We Were Not Spoiled</u>

. . . .

2. We Prepare for Our World War II Wedding

By <u>Lucille Ledoux</u> b. 1921

Our World War 2 Wedding in Maine

On Saturday evening, Mr. and Mrs. Ledoux threw us a pre-nuptial party at their home. I had known them for a long time, so they were not strangers to me. Our friends and relatives dropped by to wish us well. Mrs. Ledoux had prepared finger foods and served soft drinks and beer.

Sunday called for all the food for the reception the next day to be ready as well as for my suitcase to be packed and ready for our trip to Syracuse, NY, the next day after the wedding ceremony because Albert would have to report to base Monday night. That trip would be the only honeymoon we would have because we were having a World War 2 wedding!

My new dress was hung up with the shoes and the purse nearby for me to change into after the reception. Many people had sent money gifts as people did not have time to go shopping because of our rushed date. We did not have a rehearsal dinner—weddings were just not as big a production in those days as they are today and so we did not have a rehearsal dinner.

We were in luck that a funeral-parlor limousine was available to transport us. A chauffeur arrived at my parents' house to bring me to Holy Family. Albert was next door at his parents' and he could have driven in with me in the same car but that was not the way things were done. He must have come with his parents in their car.

Our Wedding on a Lovely Maine Day

Albert and Lucille on their wedding day, September 4th, 1944.

The wedding was at 8 on Monday morning, September 4, in the same building that I had gone to school in. (The church was downstairs and the school upstairs.) The music, provided by the chorale of girls directed by a Sister of the Presentation of Mary, began. Albert, wearing his uniform with the PFC stripes (in World War 2, men wore their uniforms for just about everything), was waiting in front with his father. My brother Paul was my ring bearer. Carrying a bouquet of white roses, I walked slowly down the aisle of the church, my arm resting in my father's bent elbow.

Once we had reached the front of the church, my father handed me over to Albert. Two chairs, each with a *prie-dieu*, had been set at the foot of the central aisle, and Albert and I took our places there.

His bother, Lucien, celebrated the Mass and preached the sermon. We had wanted him to marry us, but because of the short notice, he had not been able to get a license to marry people in Maine. Instead of Lucien, the pastor, Father Vital Nonorgues, whose Breton French accent we had grown to understand (the ceremony was conducted in French), performed the double-ring ceremony as we stood with our backs to the congregation. There are no photos of the wedding itself as cameras were not in such widespread use in those days and it was not the custom to take photos inside the church. (This made the ceremony less of a show than it is often today.)

After the Mass, because I was an *Enfant de Marie*, two *dévoileuses* (unveilers), teen-age girls from the *Enfants de Marie*, accompanied me to the altar dedicated to Mary, and we recited a prayer together. Then, they placed a crown on my head because I had been president of the *Enfants de Marie*. Then Albert and I walked down the aisle arm in arm and out to the front steps of the church.

As we exited the church, people who had lined up at the door threw rice at us. It was a lovely late-summer morning, and Albert and I posed for some informal photos. Afterwards, we went by the black limousine that had brought me and went to Laflamme Portrait Studio on Main Street to have formal pictures taken.

Our Wedding Reception

When we arrived at the *Institut Jacques Cartier* Hall, our guests—about 125 in all—were waiting for us. We did some *danses carrées* (square dancing). There were a lot of children present. We had the hall only until about 1 so after a while we sat down and had our lunch.

In the late morning, while our guests continued to chat and dance, we went home and changed. Service men in World War 2 always wore their uniforms when they traveled so Albert could stay in uniform and did not need to change. I donned my blue dress with brown accessories that I had set out earlier, and then we returned to the Jacques Cartier Hall with our luggage to say goodbye to our family and friends. From the hall on Lisbon Street, Albert and I and many of our guests went to the railroad station on Bates Street where, standing on the platform with us, my sister Gertrude cried her eyes out.

Honeymoon World War 2 Style

We left at 1:30 for Syracuse, N.Y., via Boston. Since it was still summer and the sun was out late, we saw much beautiful country as we rolled though Massachusetts and New York. When we arrived in Syracuse, it was dark. We did not have reservations for the night, so we went to the Yates Hotel downtown not far from the station. The Yates was a big hotel, and they did have a room available for us. (I don't remember if Albert had to leave me temporarily to go to the base.) We stayed at the Yates for one week. Then, we found a three-room, furnished apartment.

That's how I got married on September 4, 1944.

For more information, click here We Were Not Spoiled

. . . .

3. Albert Leaves for War, and I Go Back Home

By Lucille Ledoux b. 1921

The trip to Syracuse

We left our wedding guests at 1:30 for the train trip to Albert's base in Syracuse, N.Y. Since it was still summer and the sun was out late, we saw much beautiful country as we rolled though Massachusetts and New York. When we arrived in Syracuse, it was dark. We did not have reservations for the night, so we went to the Yates Hotel downtown not far from the station. The Yates was a big hotel, and they did have a room available for us. (I don't remember if Albert had to leave me temporarily to report to the base.)

We stayed at the Yates for one week. Then, we found a three-room, furnished apartment, which was on the same floor as two older women. We had an icebox instead of a refrigerator, and it was in the hallway. I had brought some of the sheets and towels with me that I had bought for my trousseau to go into the convent. Albert would tease me when I put the sheets on the bed. He'd say we were lying on the *draps de soeurs* (nuns sheets). All the sheets were white, and they needed ironing—not like sheets today that are permanent-press and look good without all the extra work.

I Find a Job

Since Albert was at the military base all day, I decided to find a job. Doing so was easy as there was a war going on, and there weren't enough workers. I was hired at a General Electric plant making transistors. It was good for me to get out and do something. Every morning, I took the bus to the GE plant, and Albert took another to get to the Army Air Force base, which was north of the city. He was home with me every night.

An interesting memory I have from that time was working next to an older black woman on the assembly line. Her name was Claire. I had never known a black person in Lewiston, although I had seen some, so Claire was the first one I ever talked to. She was a pleasant woman, and we got along fine although we did not become friends as I was not there long enough. The name Claire was one that I knew from home, and I thought, "If I ever have a girl, I'll call her Claire."

We Learn Unhappy News

After about five weeks, we learned that Albert was not on limited service as we had believed and that he was going to be deployed overseas. One evening, he told me he was scheduled to go to Washington State for train-ing and then he would be sent overseas. It was not a happy time for us as it meant a long separation, but during war time, we were not the only couple to face this.

Since I was already pregnant, we decided that I would stay in Syracuse until Albert left for Washington State and then I would go home to live with my parents. Without Albert, there was no reason to stay in Syracuse, since neither of us had relatives or friends there. We were both very sad to be leaving one another so soon. Albert and I would not share this pregnancy. He would miss his first child's birth. I would be having this baby all by myself. It was possible that he could be killed, and then I would be raising a child alone. Had we known he would be deployed, we would have waited to get married. Having a baby by yourself is not easy so it was fortunate my parents would be able to help me.

Albert was not permitted to go back to Lewiston with me and so he arranged for Léonard, who was nineteen, to come to pick me up. Leonard arrived with his mother in the 1940 Buick the Ledouxs had bought on my 21st birthday. So, in mid-October, after only six weeks of married life, Albert and I said goodbye to each other and, without him, I returned to Lewiston and to the room I had shared with Gertrude and Thérèse. I decided that I would continue to work as long as I could. When I went down to Benoit's, I got my job back, but I wasn't there long. The Hill Mill had gotten large government contracts to manufacture cloth for parachutes and were hiring with very good wages. I went over to the Hill Mill one day to see if they might need me, and I got hired right away as an inspector of cotton cloth on the second shift. I worked along with a number of other inspectors and our job was to examine each piece to make sure it had no defects. A bad cloth would have made a dangerous parachute for the men depending on them to land in a war zone.

In those days, there were no easy ways to communicate with people who were at a distance. Albert and I wrote to each other but the letters took a long time, it seemed to me, to arrive. I looked forward to receiving those letters from Albert, but he could not share with me some of the most important news—like where he was going to be assigned next. He had to be careful about everything he wrote in case the letter should ever fall in the wrong hands. In fact, where he was being assigned next was something he usually didn't know. The military would not tell the men where they were going. If information about where there would be reinforcements reached the enemy, this might have been dangerous for our guys.

The months go by

My pregnancy was going all right, but I missed sharing it with Albert. This was our first child, and I would have been fun to have him there with me, but that wasn't going to happen. Dr. Desaulniers kept telling me that everything about my pregnancy was all right so I wasn't worried on that account.

I was glad to be back in Lewiston but, in the back of my mind, I wondered if Albert would be safe. Would he come back home and help me raise this baby or would I be on my own, a widow?

For more information, click here We Were Not Spoiled

. . . .

Joe DiMaggio's Father Detained During WW II

Though Italian Americans were not interred, they were restricted.

C. D. Peterson b. 1937

I don't personally remember the events, but my Uncle Faust remembered and told about them all the time.

"The government was picking up Italian Americans and questioning them. Sometimes they came to peoples' houses and took away their radios and guns. Italians who were not citizens had to carry identification papers. They needed special papers to travel.

"Joe DiMaggio's father had a fishing boat in California. The government came by and wanted to arrest him because he never had become a citizen. They didn't arrest him, but they took away his fishing boat and wouldn't let him fish for months."

Uncle Faust said we shouldn't forget that Italian Americans endured their own special fearfulness.

. . . .

When the Home Front is Fort Sill, Oklahoma

Here are short clips from my home front memories.

By Peter Rostenberg, MD b. 1939

We lived in Fort Sill, Lawton, Oklahoma during WWII, while my father fought in Europe. Cherry Street, our road, ended a few houses down from us in a vast grassland; flat and far as the eye could see. While we neighborhood kids were playing outside one morning, one of us noted an undulating, wide, brown cloud developing on the horizon. It made no noise. We continued to play our cowboys and Indians until we heard a low-pitched metal-on-metal noise that seemed to be coming from beneath the cloud. It stopped us in our tracks. We ran inside to tell our mothers that something unusual was occurring, but they were not excited. Perhaps they thought it was just another Oklahoma dust cloud that would soon invade the un-airconditioned homes that summer day. We returned to our viewing booths in our front yards. The noises grew louder. We finally we saw them - tanks, halftracks, tankers, you name it! Our eyes bulged. We watched the war machines maneuver back and forth, further and closer, while telling each other, in hushed awe, what we were seeing. It all made us feel closer to the power of war. We returned to our nice, safe homes realizing how very lucky were.

Dad came home to the base on furlough, bringing with him a P38 pistol, a Mauser wrapped in cosmoline, and a huge Nazi flag. Mom was not happy. On this same furlough, Dad took us to Wichita Falls State Park to see buffalo. We found no buffalo, but I saw my first tree, standing alone in a field, not far from the road. I found the shade beneath the tree curiously cool and its grass unbelievably soft, especially for my brother John and me who usually went barefoot.

At 11 AM Mass I would put my head on my mother's lap to rest and wait for the Cherokee women who came to church wearing the beautiful, bright hand crafted blankets. I understand Oklahoma was 20% native American at that time. And finally, at the commissary, I would walk to the back where supplies were delivered to watch the rail road tracks. I waited for the steam engines to emerge, rushing out from the low woods and when they did, it made my day…nothing could be more exciting than that!

On our way back east, we drove into the late dusk toward Oklahoma City. We finally found a motel comprised of separate little houses. I wondered why all the other motels were full, but this one had lots of vacancies. Just before falling asleep, with lights out, we discovered the reason for so few customers: We were located near the end of a military air strip. Planes took off right above our heads.

It's funny what you remember about the war time home front.

The War Altered Even Simple Choices

A small corner of life on the home front copes with the effects of WW II.

Don Bracken b. 1935

During the war, patriotic songs were made popular on the radio. Some related directly to the troops, sailors and airmen.

One Sunday morning, during the usual performance of hymns at a children's service, someone requested something patriotic but religious too, like "Praise the Lord and Pass the Ammunition." The priest, probably weighing in his mind the morality issue of praying to God for help in the killing of another human being, thought for a moment and came up with "Coming In On a Wing and a Prayer." We settled for that.

. . . .

A Child's Long Island Home Front

George Rodgers b. 1933

The 1930s were challenging years for my Mother and Father, they were beginning to recover from the depression. We lived in an attached house, or row of attached houses in Jackson Heights, on Long Island, NY. Standing on the front steps we could see the passengers looking out the windows as their DC-3 airliners that were landing at La Guardia Airport. Mother said she could see the ladies putting on their make-up.

One day, shortly before Christmas Mother was taking me into "the city" (as they called New York). It was snowing as we walked to the subway.

HOME FRONT

While passing one row house, the family was moving their furniture out on the front lawn. It bothered me, and I asked my Mother why they we doing that on a snowy day. She bent down and whispered. "They didn't pay their rent and they are being evicted from their home." This really up`set me. What would happen to these people?

Could that happen to us? This was my first touch with life's realities. And there was nothing I could do to help this family, or my own.

One Sunday afternoon I was allowed to play with my lead soldiers in the living room. There was an artificial fire place where I was positioning my troops among the logs. Mother and Dad were sitting with my sister listening to the radio. It was a wonderful feeling to be with them and have my favorite toys, too.

After a while, there was a news flash that interrupted the radio program, "The Japanese have attacked Pearl Harbor……."

After much shock and amazed adult conversation my father said,

"This means war……"

My father at 40, married with two children, was not an immediate candidate for the draft. However, he tried to join the Navy offering his experience planning the loading of cargo, which was what he did for American Steel Export Company. But, the Navy physical revealed a heart murmur, so he tried the Army (who ran their own supply corps freighters). It looked like the Army would take Dad, so our row house was sold and we sat up all night on a train called "The Silver Meteor" going to Miami.

Dad rented an Apartment over a garage on Lincoln Avenue and we awaited his orders. All the major hotels were taken over by the Army. I was thrilled to see real live soldiers marching in the street, calling out cadence. This went on all day, and the golf courses had them drilling with rifles. However, I was disappointed that they were not firing them.

On rare occasions we went out to diner where the grownups raved about Florida red snapper followed by key lime pie.

The best part was I did not have to go to school, but after a couple of months the Army discovered Dad's heart problem, and turned him down.

So, back we went to Long Island, but this time to Centerport, a village about 60 miles from NYC. Dad commuted leaving at 6:00 AM (returning about 7:00 PM) daily planning cargo loads for the same company he worked for earlier, but now his customer was Uncle Sam.

We followed the War with maps of the Allied and Axis forces struggle published in the newspapers. Several of Dad's business friends were caught up in the fall of Shanghai, Singapore, and Hong Kong. There was bad news all over the world. London was being bombed and the news reels show fires and buildings toppling down. Germany was advancing all over the world, even in North Africa. Japan captured the Philippines and we heard terrible stories about the "Bataan Death March".

Then there was a wonderful event shown on the movie theater newsreels. U.S. Army bombers could be seen staggering into the air, taking off our Navy's aircraft carrier Hornet....Jimmy Doolittle thrilled the world leading an attack bombing Tokyo !

Months later Dad received Capt. Ted Lawson's Book of the Month Club selection "Thirty Seconds over Tokyo". I still have it.

Next, came the jungle war in Guadalcanal. A high school class mate of my sister's was wounded there, and was shipped home in time for his graduation.

When the Battle of Midway took place the newsreels showed the carries and their aircraft in exciting action. For me, and my friends, this was more than "visual history", it was the "wild west" at sea. We learned the names of our carriers. During any free time in school we would draw airplanes firing on the enemy aircraft and ships. We used rulers to draw strait lines of our fire.

As kids, all of our lives were involved in war. I even remember the comics featuring Terry & the Pirates and Steve Canyon, fighting for China against the invading Japanese, before Pearl Harbor. Madame Chiang Kai-shek was schooled in the US and toured the country promoting support for China. It was all very romantic,

Eventually, the big day arrived. People went to church to pray for the troops landing on "D Day" the 5th of June 1944. The news reels of the landings were frightening, and the death on the beach was very real. But the day by day advance of the Allied Forces appeared on the front page of newspapers. Victory in Europe seemed to be on the way.

The Pacific War featured island hopping invasions with Marines storming ashore under deadly fire. Despite heavy naval bombardments, the resistance was heavy and the losses were terrible. Flame throwers made war look horrible, but we had to win.

Then one night our family went to the movies to see the first newsreel of the Atomic Bomb dropped on Hiroshima. That was shocking, but it made the war end, and everyone we knew was thrilled.

George announcing himself c. 1941

. . . .

Me, My Father, and World War II

My memories of World War II revolve around my father.

Carol Ann Cullom b. 1935

He was a corporal in the Army. We knew he was 'overseas' but we didn't always know where. I worried that he might get hurt, or worse. I was in the third grade at Woodrow Wilson School when one day he surprised me by walking up to me on the playground. He was wearing his uniform. The kids all crowded around. I cried.

I hated to see his furlough end. A short time after he went back, John Spence's father was killed. I worried with fear every day and night after that until my father finally came back home when the war ended. It was just before Christmas. I have been grateful for that all my life.

. . . .

The Songs of the 40s

I can still hear them

- they provided the background of the era

by Bob Saulnier b. 1928

Reflecting on the subject of the WWII home front and what we who were there remember most vividly, I suddenly realized that one of the features that meant so much to me was - the *music* - the many great songs that were produced by the dozen, played and sung by the "big bands" and vocalists - the milkman - the barber - and me. I seem to remember them all. They played a big part in boosting public morale, making the "war effort" more personal and acceptable; inspiring us to fight the enemy, and softening the pain of personal separations. Here are some of those that come to mind easily:

The war - the enemy - the effort:

"They started something - we're gonna end it - right in their own backyard..."

"We did it before and we can do it again - and we will do it again...."

"The Victory Polka"

"Remember Pearl Harbor"

"Right in der Feuhrer's Face"

"Goodby, Mama, I'm Off to Yokohama"

"There'll be a Hot Time in Berlin"

"Any Bonds Today?"

"White Cliffs of Dover"

"Comin' in on a Wing and a Prayer" (though there's one motor gone, we can still carry on....")

"We'll Fill the Air With Eagles (we'll fill the clouds with men...)

"Praise the Lord and Pass the Ammunition"

"Private Roger Young" (fought and died for the men he marched among)

The boys — life in military:

"This is the Army, Mr. Jones (no private rooms or telephones..."

"Dear Mom (the weather today was cloudy and damp....miss you)

"I Have Your PIcture by my Bed....."

"Don't Sit Under the Apple Tree with Anyone Else But Me"

"Some Day I'm Gonna Murder the Bugler....

"Move it Over" (said the private to the sergeant,' all the buttons on my coat are gone - said the sergeant to the private, "I will sew them on...."

Home - personal - future:

"We'll Meet Again (don't know where, don't know when..."

"Bell Bottom Trousers, Coat of Navy Blue"

"A Boy in Khaki, a GIrl in Lace"

"Three Little Sisters (one loved a a soldier, one loved a sailor and one loved a guy in the Marines)

"PS - I Love You"

"He Wears a Pair of Silver Wings"

"I Came Here to Talk for Joe"

"The Stage Door Canteen"

Others:

"Johnny Doughboy Found a Rose in Ireland"

"There's a Star-spangled Banner Waving Somewhere" (crippled boy begging recruiter to take him)

"How're You Gonna Keep 'em Happy Down on the Farm after they've seen Paree?"

****

These and other colorful, stimulating tunes 'struck a note' - even now, running the lyrics through my mind, the memories return... a 'paperboy' who delivered the war news door-to-door - and became a veteran of WW II, fresh from high school.

. . . .

An interview with Mr. Samuel Hyman

A Civil Rights Activist

b. 1938

Were the war time experiences of black people different from those of whites? The basis for the interview was to examine the question, at least from the viewpoint of one individual. Sam felt that at the all-encompassing level - war, separation, rationing, fear, making do and so on

- experiences were probably no different. However, he saw important differences in the impact, especially in the post-war era and beyond.

For Sam, who grew on a farm in North Carolina, one war time practice did remain vivid. German prisoners of war were used in the south to work on farms. They were transported by train from whatever detention center held them to the farm owners' locations by train. The German prisoners were escorted in their own rail car, while the era's Jim Crow rules forbid blacks from even riding in the same car as the white prisoners, and had to ride in cars behind them.

On the civilian front, political and labor struggles for black rights kicked into high gear as the war effort wound up. The demand for labor worked as a force for gaining better conditions. Many steps forward were taken during the war.

The young black men who volunteered served in all phases of the war, but often were assigned jobs as drivers, cooks, truck drivers and even grave diggers. While some of the skills, such as cooking, working with vehicles, and cargo handling were useful in civilian life, few gained technical or administrative skills. None the less, these young men had seen new and different ways of life and their expectations and goals had been altered. The G. I. Bill gave the returnees a means to seek out other futures that they had never considered.

Many went back to high school and then moved, most often at night, the new spate of technical and trade schools that sprang up to meet demand - and respond to the government paid tuition.

The trade schools played an important role because it led many of the veterans into trade roles as plumbers, carpenters and builders and eventually into their own businesses. Sam believes this extension into entrepreneurship simply wouldn't have happened as quickly without the G.I. Bill.

Many black veterans who Sam remembers, used the benefits to attend college and often chose careers as teachers or in government, particularly in the post office. Many other careers still remained closed to them. The pursuit of government jobs often meant a migration to Washington DC, forming the basis of today's heavy black population in that city.

The VA loan program that accompanied the G. I. Bill provided the funds for the veterans to become first time home owners. This higher demand, coupled with the growth in black construction and entrepreneurship, along with the VA loan program, helped to create a new community of ownership. "Without the VA loan program this would not have happened for another generation," Sam said.

There were other spillover effects of the war on black veterans which resulted from the country's huge surge in demand for goods and services. Many veterans were drawn to Detroit's auto plants and to the manufacturing factories clustered around cities in the Mid-west and Northeast, adding to a general black migration already underway.

Sam explained a special by-product of blacks' war time service - pride. "The veterans demonstrated their pride in their service by wearing their uniforms around town. They had played their role in winning the war. They felt honor in their victory. The community shared that pride just like communities all over the country. Their earned pride expanded into earned expectations to be treated just like other communities."

"The history and impact of this era on all of us should not be forgotten," Sam said.

C. D. PETERSON

The Home Front Round Table

In September 2017, fifteen wonderful seniors agreed to sit and share their memories of the war years on the home front. We met at the Elmwood Hall / Danbury Senior Center in Danbury, Connecticut. The Director who brought us together is Susan M. Tomanio, LCSW

My strongest impression came to me a few hours after the session when I realized that no one was surprised at what the others had said. World War II was truly a shared experience for this generation of Americans. The fifteen people sitting around the table had an understood, unspoken bond. "The war was our life," they said matter-of-factly.

December 7th itself did not produce the vivid recollections I imagined it would. Most were young in 1941. One woman attended a concert that evening and was startled when the orchestra broke into the Star Spangled Banner. One man remembered a vaudeville show that hastily changed its presentation.

A man who grew up in New Haven said that it seemed that some sort of defense plan must have been in place all along. He recalled how quickly sentries appeared and how soon restrictions were placed along the waterfront where navy vessels anchored.

Rationing was discussed as if it happened yesterday. "Oh, yes, we traded stamps and often had to make do with what we had," one woman said with no bitterness. One woman recalled that because nylon stockings weren't available, some women simply painted a seam line down the back of their legs. (I wonder now how many women today even know that nylons once had seams.)

All of them remembered air raid drills. "If the drill was planned," one woman said, "It meant the girls could wear slacks."

When I asked if they were afraid during the drills, they paused and looked around at each other and each said one version or another of, "No, we were all just doing what we were supposed to do." A former professional baseball player in the group said there was one thing that scared him and that was when they turned on search lights reaching way up into the sky. He felt they had to mean some kind of trouble. Another man remembered that during blackouts he was sometimes home alone, with no flashlight and that frightened him.

The words "doing what we were supposed to do" struck me as almost outdated. When I mentioned my observation, several wondered if we, as a country could ever have that sense of togetherness and duty again. One woman quickly pointed out that we did have a moment of that unity after 9/11.

Doing what we were supposed to do back then included collecting scrap metal, even if it meant prowling the woods to find it. Some collected pots and pans, others collected paper, some collected fat drippings and everyone collected tin foil!

Every one chuckled when we tried to think of whatever happened to all that tin foil. We rolled it into balls and the ball got bigger when we brought it into school, then it got bigger at the collection center, but none of us knew where it went from there. We were all sure it went for a grand cause, but supposed the whole collection activity might have been a way just to keep us occupied and feeling like we were contributing to the war effort. One woman contributed to the war effort by making "ditty bags." I neglected to ask what was put into the bags.

War bonds and stamps were a shared memory. One man remembered exactly that once a person had saved up $18.75 in stamps, the book could be traded in for a $25 War Bond. One participant's memories did jar me. She pointed out that many, if not most people, did not have telephones. A Western Union bicycle delivery boy was a common sight. (While I grew up before television, we always had a telephone.) Telegrams, radio, and the movies provided their information about the war. For most, it wasn't a household topic, except for worry over a loved one. Most did not remember the war being discussed a lot in school, though one man recalled that a teacher had a wall map of Europe marked with pins denoting action.

One woman remembered that the movie theaters ran bond drives. A short feature would have a movie star urging patrons to buy bonds and savings stamps. Then the theater lights would come up and ushers would come around to collect.

A man started the topic of women in the war by referring to the iconic Rosie the Riveter. He also reminded the group of the brave women who ferry- piloted war planes from the U.S. to England. A woman who grew up in Philadelphia described her role executing classified contracts for radar procurement. The group acknowledged that women being drawn into the workforce marked a big change and that these women were often met with prejudice both during and after the war.

We did not inter our German Americans or our Italian Americans, but one man recalled that in the Italian neighborhoods of his youth, Italians were interrogated about their families in Italy. Several spoke about the Nazi German Bund movement which, held meetings in New York City and very nearby Danbury, but curiously, no one could recall what happened, if anything, to their members.

The sadness of separation did not come up, though one man said he almost never saw his father who had two defense jobs and was also an air raid warden. The mention of Christmas did not bring forth anything special from this group. Bread was baked, carols sung, Macy's visited and electric trains unwrapped.

The meeting's final topic concerned the impact of the war on people. "We and our enemies did awful things to each other, "one man said. "We seem to forget and go to war again every 20 years." A woman remarked about the hideous propaganda posters she recalled. Everyone seemed to remember someone who came home with battle fatigue or "shell shocked" as it was called. "We saw a lot of alcoholism after the war," a woman noted. "You can't go through something like that and not be affected."

"The effects of war go on for a long time," one woman said. "I watched some of the first holocaust survivors come to New York City. They were barely able to cope." Then she explained. "I saw it affect them, their children and their children's children."

The Seniors

Carl Tomanio, Lydia Tomanio, William Seymour, Eleanor Preisig, Joan Gall, Gerry Ulich, Gil Black, Dolores Morganthaler, Robert Wolfe, Bob Saulnier, Mario Tomanio, Walter Stanley Doris Lubin, and Sondra Schneider

. . . .

HOME FRONT

C. D. Peterson

Coming of age in the 1940s and early 50s, the author is among the
who personally experienced the scarcity of the depression, the patriot
during World War II and the exuberance in that brief, post-war per
when we felt safe and when the middle class was born.

Married for more than 50 years, he is the proud father of thr
fascinating children. Raised on his family's dairy farm, he is a
MIT graduate, a former Navy pilot, and a dedicated fly fisherman
He has written five books on business subjects and a full scale history. Hi
work includes pieces about fly fishing, a published poem and an award
winning song. His essays have been published in several newspapers.

. . . .

To have your story included in my blog please go to

www.homefrontmemoir.com

ee
n
.
s

Made in the USA
Columbia, SC
30 May 2018